BEYOND
THE VEIL

BEYOND
THE VEIL

By
Boyce Mouton

With Introduction
By
Knofel Staton

Printed and bound in
United States of America

International Standard Book Number: 0-89900-314-1

NO RIGHTS RESERVED

. . . As His Spirit leads

. . . And for God's glory

. . . You are encouraged to use this material

. . . For the building up of His Body

. . . And for the evangelization of the world

TABLE OF CONTENTS

INTRODUCTION

There is hardly any difference between a God who is dead and a God who is impotent.

But our God is neither.

Christianity has done a great disservice to the nature of God by pretending that God shelved His power when either the apostles died or when the last book of the Bible was written.

We have done global evangelism a disservice by sending missionaries to places where the devil has been actively involved in manifesting his power to tell the good news about a god who checked in His power at the end of the first century. They tell about a god who had power then, but not power today. Do we really think that people will give up the gods with their powers for the true God with no power?

Boyce Mouton in this book has shown contemporary evidences that God is still alive and active.

The true events in this book should not surprise us. After all, there is no such thing as "natural" laws that govern this planet. All of the laws are "supernatural." God created them and thus can go beyond them or intervene in them any time He wishes without bringing imbalance. He has said, "I have made the laws that control earth and sky" (Jer. 33:25, TEV). And we read, "all things remain to this day because of your command, because they are all your servants" (Ps. 119:91). Did you catch that? All of creation are servants of God. He is the Master. Consequently, "He gives a command to the earth and what He says is quickly done" (Ps. 147:15, TEV). And "by His command they were fixed in the places forever, and they cannot disobey" (Ps. 148:6, TEV).

That is why God could command the sun to stand still and it obeyed. What He really did was cause the earth to quit its rotation for awhile; yet nothing got out of balance. He is the Master. He can command a storm to stop. He can command lions' mouths to close. He can command the flames not to burn in a furnace. He can command a fish to swallow a man and then later command that fish to spit him out on the dry land. That is a powerful God!

Our prayers affect God. He is a Father who is pleased when we pray and delights to hear us pray. And God changes His mind in direct response to the prayers of His people (Exod. 32:9-14, 2 Kings 20:1-8, Amos 7:3, 6, Jonah 4:1, 2). After all, that is partly what it means when we pray "Our Father *who art in Heaven.*" He is not trapped by circumstances, environment, the "laws" of earth. He is above it all and is indeed in control of what He has created.

Some readers may be uncomfortable and then ask, "why do these wonderful things happen to those people but not to me?"

Through the years, we have probably asked our parents the same question in essence. The answer is not that God is a respecter of persons, nor is it that God loves some people less than others. His love is everlasting and inclusive. Nor is the answer God does not care. He cares for all.

We must allow God to be God with all of His mercy, love, wisdom, and power. We will never be able to answer the why's except to affirm that "His ways and His thoughts are far above ours as the heavens are above the earth."

One thing is certain. We must not try to capture the power of God for our self-centered interests. God has made it clear to us that our life on earth is temporary. We are all like vapor; we are in the process of dying. We must not become so attached to this world, this body, this life that our expectations of God's intervention is primarily because we love the now too much to let it go.

Boyce Mouton's book reminds us of two important truths: God is God with all of the power that belongs to Him. Man is man with all the perplexities that belong to us.

Let's let God be God. Let's commit ourselves to be His people, depending upon Him with faith and serving Him with love.

Knofel Staton

A "HOW TO" BOOK?

This is a book about the supernatural. There is a possibility that by reading these words your faith will grow and your understanding of God will deepen. Because of this God may choose to use you in some new dimension or capacity which is now beyond your wildest imagination.

This is, however, not a "How To" book in the traditional sense of the word. God is not Someone whom we can manipulate or control by human pressure and finite reasoning. He is the Sovereign of the universe to Whom we offer our unconditional surrender. We need to pray like Job: "Though He slay me, yet will I trust Him" (Job 13:15).

Even if it were possible for us to do all of the things which God commands us to do we would still need to confess; "We are unprofitable servants: we have done that which was our duty to do" (Luke 17:10).

Our boldness and confidence to enter in beyond the veil do not come from the merits of human achievement, but from the blood of Jesus Christ. This new and living way has been consecrated for us through the veil, that is to say, His flesh.

Let us prepare to enter in!

PREFACE

The purpose of a veil is to cover or conceal. The first use of this word in the Bible is Genesis 24:65. When Rebekah lifted up her eyes and saw Isaac, The Scriptures state that ". . . she took a veil, and covered herself."

The next use of the word in Scripture is found in association with Tamar who used a veil to conceal her identity from the unsuspecting Judah. He even fathered a child by Tamar without recognizing her true identity, for she was covered with a veil (Gen. 38:14, 19).

The next time the Holy Bible mentions a veil is in association with the Tabernacle (Exod. 26:31),

> And thou shalt make a veil of blue and purple, and scarlet, and fine twined linen of cunning work: with cherubims shall it be made . . .

15

This veil was to hang before the Holy of Holies to conceal that room from the world outside.

Each time a veil was used it was to conceal something!

THE FLESH OF JESUS WAS A VEIL

Having therefore, brethren, boldness to enter into the holiest by the blood of Jesus, By a new and living way, which he hath consecrated for us, through the veil, that is to say, his flesh . . . (Heb. 10:19-20).

The spiritual implications of this verse are far-reaching and revolutionary. It causes us to reassess our total perspective of the Life of Christ on earth.

There is obviously a sense in which Jesus came to "reveal" God. This is the literal meaning of the word "revelation." It signifies to "draw back" as a curtain or unveil that which has been concealed.

The Scriptures teach that Jesus came to "declare" God.

No man hath seen God at any time; the only begotten Son, which is in the bosom of the Father, he hath declared him (John 1:18).

The Greek word translated in this verse as "declared" is "exegomai" which literally means to "lead out." It is the basis of our English word "exegete" which means to "explain." An exegetical sermon, for example, is one which merely explains a passage of Scripture.

Jesus came to "explain" God. But God is a Spirit. There is therefore a sense in which the flesh of Jesus needs to be drawn aside that we might truly see God.

IT IS POSSIBLE TO KNOW JESUS IN THE FLESH AND YET NOT KNOW GOD.

Perhaps no people on the face of the earth were more familiar with the fleshly Jesus than were His neighbors in Nazareth.

They had lived with Him for almost thirty years. They knew the members of His family by name. As a matter of fact, they were so familiar with the flesh of Jesus, that they found it all but impossible to see the nature of His miracle working power.

It seems that there in Nazareth, where people were more familiar with the flesh of Jesus than anywhere else on earth, He had the greatest difficulty penetrating into the world of the supernatural. Mark states it succinctly:

> And He could there (at Nazareth) do no mighty work, save that he laid his hands upon a few sick folk, and healed them. And He marvelled because of their unbelief . . . (Mark 6:5-6).

But the problem of knowing Jesus from only the fleshly point of view was not unique to His neighbors in Nazareth. It was a problem also for His closest friends.

The night before Jesus was crucified, Philip, one of His disciples, said to Him in the upper room: "Lord, show us the Father and it sufficeth us" (John 14:8).

Jesus answered: "Have I been so long time with you, and yet hast thou not known me, Philip? He that hath seen me hath seen the Father . . ."

These words are both interesting and profound. Philip certainly knew Jesus in the flesh. He could recognize the fleshly Jesus in a crowd of many thousands, which in fact he did on many occasions.

Moreover, Philip knew virtually every Bible story which is recorded in the four Gospels. He could tell you about the Samaritan woman at Jacob's well, the ten lepers, the healing of the Nobleman's son, etc.

Yet, it is obvious that Philip had missed something very significant.

Again we remind you that the flesh of Jesus Christ is called a veil. The Greek word so translated in Hebrews 10:19 is "katapetasma." This is the very word used of that veil between the Holy Place and the Holy of Holies.

17

The Old Testament priests could memorize that veil without ever spending one moment in the presence of God. They could draw a likeness of the cherubim and explain every beautiful color and intricate design without ever having the thrill of a first-hand experience with Deity. They could interrogate the High Priest about his experience, but they could have no personal experience of their own.

In the same way, it is possible for people today to memorize Bible facts and study Bible stories without ever meeting Jesus face to face in the intimate experience of conversion.

THE LIFE OF CHRIST

If you were to enroll in a class on the "Life of Christ" you would probably expect to start with the story of the nativity in Bethlehem and conclude with the resurrection and ascension. This story basically covers a period of some 33 years.

In reality, the Life of Christ has no beginning or end. Jesus existed before there was a single atom of creation or even an angel to revolt in heavenly places. As a matter of fact, the Scriptures teach explicitly that Jesus created everything, and without Him was not anything made that was made (John 1:3).

Neither does the life of Christ conclude with His ascension from Mt. Olivet. The Gospels only record what Jesus "began to do and teach" (Acts 1:1). Jesus is alive and well today . . . and praise God, He will never die! The book of Acts describes what Jesus did in the lives of men like Peter and Paul.

BOLDNESS TO ENTER IN

There is a dramatic difference between the age of Law and the age of Grace. The devout Jew not only would never think of entering beyond the veil, he would not even attempt to pronounce the name of God. The name Jehovah, therefore, was an ineffable name, or a name too sacred to even be spoken.

The Christian, by contrast, rushes boldly into the Holiest of all and cries out to God with the most intimate terms of endearment, "Abba, Father."

In this regard there are many Christians who are living B.C. lives in an A.D. world. They can recite from memory every fleshly story about Jesus, but they have never had an intimate experience beyond the veil. They can see a two-dimensional Jesus like a curtain before God, but they fear to enter into that new dimension which confronts God in the here and now. They feel comfortable with the concept that Christ is safely tucked away in a little cubical 33 years by 33 years by 33 years, but they fear to step through that veil of the flesh and experience the personal glory which causes our bodies to become temples of the Holy Spirit, and our own hearts the Ark of His blessed Covenant.

If you have a spirit of fear, you did not get it from God, for God hath not given us a spirit of fear, but of power, and of love, and of a sound mind (II Tim. 1:7).

THE NEED FOR BALANCE

Technically speaking, a clock is only accurate when its pendulum is in the middle. When the pendulum is at one extreme, the gear which it controls is locked in place and the clock is a fraction too slow. When the pendulum is at the other extreme, the clock is a fraction too fast. Technically speaking, the clock is only accurate when the pendulum is in the middle.

Certainly, the Bible is an inspired and accurate record of God's revelation to man. It is profitable for doctrine, reproof, correction, and instruction in righteousness. Every Christian would certainly be well advised to sink spiritual roots deep into the Sacred Scriptures.

Yet, the Scriptures do not deal specifically with every question which confronts the child of God. The principles of Scripture will certainly help you in selecting a job, choosing a mate, etc.,

19

but the specific answers to our personal problems demand a new dimension with Deity.

The Bible teaches:

> If any of you lack wisdom, let him ask of God, that giveth to all men liberally, and upbraideth not; and it shall be given him. But let him ask in faith, nothing wavering. For he that wavereth is like a wave of the sea driven with the wind and tossed. For let not that man think that he shall receive any thing of the Lord. A double-minded man is unstable in all his ways . . . (James 1:5-8).

If we forget our spiritual roots and do not ground ourselves in the Word of God, there is the ever-present danger that we might wind up following some false prophet.

Such a danger should never dissuade us, however, from obeying the Scriptural injunction to enter in boldly into the Holiest of all by the blood of Jesus. When we pray, we must pray boldly . . . nothing doubting.

LIGHT AND DARKNESS

A friend once wrote a booklet on the subject of grace. He was criticized by a colleague who feared that someone would turn such teaching into license. In the discussion which followed, they concluded that any time we teach about grace in such a way that no one can misunderstand, we are teaching it differently than Paul did. The true teaching about grace will leave open the possibility that some unstable soul may believe that they should do evil that good may come, or that they should continue in sin that grace might abound. God forbid! The Scriptures do not teach such abominations . . . but they do teach grace in such a way that some people thought that they did.

To state the same truth in another way, every time we try to protect light we produce darkness.

Thus, when we teach about God working in our own day and age, we are running the risk that someone will abuse this teaching to their own destruction.

The obedient believer, however, does not have an option! We are commanded to enter into the Holiest by the blood of Jesus . . . and we are commanded to enter in boldly.

If we try to protect this beautiful light, we shall only produce shadows which will prove much more dangerous than light. We are not children of the night who love darkness; we are children of the day who love light.

The Scriptures teach in I Corinthians 7 that to avoid fornication, every man is to have his own woman and every woman is to have her own man. When men and women are denied a legitimate way to express their most intimate desires, they will frequently wind up in perversion or other forms of immorality.

So also in the world of the Spirit, when Christian people are denied a proper expression of their most intimate spiritual desires, they are sometimes driven to extremes which harm the Body of Christ and hurt the cause of world evangelism. Just as perversion sometimes rears its ugly head on board a ship at sea where men are denied a normal contact with their wives, a perversion of the Gospel will sometimes break out like fire in the most dead and dry of denominations.

YOUR PERSONAL INVITATION

Since the veil of the temple was rent in twain, the Holy Bible invites you to enter in boldly for a personal encounter with Deity. It is not necessary for you to merely listen to someone else tell you what it is like to be in the presence of God, to have answers to prayer, or to operate on a power that is able to do exceeding abundantly above all that we can ask or think. You have a personal invitation from God to enter in yourself.

This little book is written with the hope and prayer that it will provide you with information and inspiration to help you enter in. Christ did not just come that you might have life—but life abundant.

I

BEYOND THE VEIL

And there I will meet with thee, and I will commune with thee from above the mercy seat, from between the two cherubims which are upon the ark of the testimony . . . (Exod. 25:22).

When God gave instructions regarding the building of a Tabernacle, He began by telling them how to construct the Ark of the Covenant. This was to be the central item of furniture in the Tabernacle, and the very hub around which Hebrew worship would revolve.

It was here, between the outstretched wings of the cherubim, that God would meet with His people. The Hebrews were not permitted to erect an altar at any other place in the world. Wherever the winds of fortune might carry them, they were required to return to the location of the Ark of the Covenant in order that they might worship God (Deut. 12:5).

Instructions regarding the building of the ark are found in Exodus 25:10-22. It was a rectangular box made out of acacia wood and overlaid with pure gold. The dimensions of the ark are given in the Bible in cubits. Translated into more familiar measurements, it was about 3 3/4 feet long, 2 1/4 feet wide, and 2 1/4 feet high.

The ark was fashioned with golden rings at each corner through which were inserted gold plated poles of acacia wood. These poles were never to be removed and were the instruments by which the ark was to be transported (Exod. 25:12-15).

On top of the ark was a golden slab called the "mercy seat." At each end of the mercy seat were angelic figures called "cherubim." The cherubim were facing each other with their outstretched wings overshadowing the mercy seat and their faces gazing toward the mercy seat.

The ark was constructed by gifted individuals like Bezaleel and Aholiab (Exod. 31:1-7). It was to be the container for the Ten Commandments which constituted the Covenant which God made with Israel. It also contained a golden pot of manna and Aaron's rod that budded (Heb. 9:4). Later it would also become the receptacle for the book of the law which was placed in its side shortly before the death of Moses (Deut. 31:26).

Once constructed, the ark was placed in the innermost sanctuary of the Tabernacle, called the "holy of holies." From this time onward, it was never to be seen by anyone that survived, other than the High Priest . . . and he could only gaze upon it one day per year.

The ark was placed behind an ornate veil and anyone who disregarded that veil died in the process. The men of Bethshemesh, for example, dared to look into the ark of the covenant and perished (I Sam. 6:19).

The High Priest, if properly sanctified and clothed, was permitted to approach the ark on the Day of Atonement. A part of his apparel included a robe of blue, purple, and scarlet which was also adorned with golden bells (Exod. 28:33-34). These bells provided those listening outside with proof that the High Priest was alive. Should he die in the Holy of Holies,

24

tradition tells us that a rope was fastened to his leg so that his body might be retrieved. No one but the High Priest was permitted to enter into the Holy of Holies for any reason.

When the Tabernacle was moved and the ark had to be transported, it was to be covered at all times. First of all, the tent was collapsed in such a way that the ark was covered by the veil separating the Holy of Holies from the Holy Place (Num. 4:5). Then it was to be also covered by skins and a blue cloth (Num. 4:6).

You can well imagine the curiosity that must have abounded as men pondered what it was like to meet with God beyond the veil. They could not know, however, for such an experience was forbidden to them.

They could read about the ark in the Bible . . . but they could not experience it firsthand. They could interrogate the High Priest about his impressions and experiences, but they could not enjoy those experiences and impressions themselves. All they could ever have would be the testimony of someone else.

Then came that glorious day when Jesus opened up a new and living way into the presence of God.

> The veil of the temple was rent in twain from the top to the bottom and the earth did quake, and the rocks rent (Matt. 27:51).

The veil was not opened by human wisdom and the strategy of men. It was rent from the "top to the bottom" by the power of God.

Surely you can relate to the mixed emotions of those Jewish priests who ministered in the Holy Place that day. All of their lives they must have wondered what it really looked like behind the veil. Now for the first time in their lives they had an opportunity to look . . . but many of them, I'm sure, were not able.

Their curiosity was mingled with fear. Just what if God should smite them dead as He did the men of Bethshemesh? Just what if God should cause them to perish as He did Uzzah (II Sam. 6)? Just what if they should contract leprosy as did Uzziah (II Chron. 26:19)?

I confess to you that there was a time in my life when I would have been terrified to even glance at the gaping tear in the sacred veil. I would have stared at the ground or deliberately faced the other way.

Yet, today I am challenged by the realization that God hath not given us a spirit of fear (II Tim. 1:7). He did not give us the Law as a permanent barrier to restrict our lives forever; it was only a schoolmaster to bring us unto Christ that we might be justified by faith (Gal. 3:24).

In Christ we possess a certain boldness which comes from the Holy Spirit. The Jewish rabbi would stand afar off and not even pronounce the name of Jehovah . . . the Christian draws near with confidence into the very presence of God and cries out "Abba, Father."

Our next chapter contains an incredible story. I am personnally convinced it is true . . . even though the essence of the story cannot be found in the Scriptures.

Brace yourself for "First Glances" beyond the veil.

THOUGHT QUESTIONS FOR CHAPTER I

1. Why was God so secretive during the days of the Law?
2. Why was God so severe with people who did not respect the "veil" of His secrecy?
3. Discuss the commandment not to take the name of the Lord our God in vain with the Jewish refusal to even pronounce the name of Jehovah.
4. How is the Christian emboldened to call God "Abba" or "Daddy" (Gal. 4:6)?
5. How can a serious student serve God with boldness and without fear since the fear of the Lord is the beginning of knowledge (see Prov. 1:7 and II Tim. 1:7)?
6. If you had been in the Holy Place when Jesus died, would you have looked beyond the veil?

7. What would give you "boldness" to enter in beyond the veil?
8. Why would some be afraid even today to enter beyond the veil?
9. How can they be helped?
10. What does it mean to you to "enter into the holiest by the blood of Jesus"?

II

FIRST GLANCES

That saith of Cyrus, He is my shepherd, and shall perform all my pleasure: even saying to Jerusalem, Thou shalt be built; and to the temple, Thy foundation shall be laid. Thus saith the Lord to his anointed, to Cyrus, whose right hand I have holden, to subdue nations before him; and I will loose the loins of kings, to open before him the two leaved gates; and the gates shall not be shut (Isa. 44:28—45:1).

Our first glances behind the veil will perhaps be hesitant and tentative. We will be reluctant to stare very long for fear that we might be contaminated.

Our observations will be distinguished from viewing only the Scriptures. Believing that the Scriptures are inspired of God, we accept them regardless of evidence which seems to the contrary. There are literally hundreds, and perhaps thousands of instances where men once thought the Bible to be wrong, only to discover through better research and additional information that the Bible was right and its critics were wrong.

When we look beyond the veil, however, we will be probing into areas about which the Bible gives no specific information. Certainly there are dangers to be avoided, yet we are promised a certain "boldness" to enter into the Holiest by the blood of Christ. This is a new and living way, which he hath consecrated for us, "through the veil, that is to say His flesh . . ."

Therefore, let us look "beyond the veil" or "behind the scenes" at Cyrus. By doing so we will be probing into someone's personal experience as opposed to studying a passage of Scripture.

It is a fact that the book of Isaiah mentions a conqueror named Cyrus who would authorize the building of Jerusalem and the laying of the foundation of the temple. At this time, however, Jerusalem and the temple had not yet even been destroyed.

Isaiah lived in the eighth century before Christ. His prophetic ministry came during the reigns of Uzziah, Jotham, Ahaz, and Hezekiah (Isa. 1:1). If he began his ministry while in his twenties, he would have been over eighty years of age when Hezekiah died.

Cyrus, about whom he wrote these predictive prophecies, would not even be born until about 600 B.C.

Most children are expected only nine months before their birth, but the world expected Cyrus generations before he was conceived in his mother's womb.

Keil and Delitzsch observe that Cyrus is the only Gentile king whom Jehovah has called His "anointed."

Thus, we have some remarkable facts which cannot be gain-said or controverted, and the more deeply we probe, the more amazing the story becomes.

Since both Jesus and Cyrus are called the Lord's anointed, we should not be surprised to discover some similarities surrounding the circumstances of their entrance into the world.

In particular, we would point out the desire of Satan to have both of these babies killed, and thus thwart the plan of God and keep His prophetic truths from coming to pass.

30

The name Cyrus is the Latin form of the old Persian word "Kurush" and is applied to three prominent men in history.

Cyrus I - the son of Teispes and grandfather of Cyrus the Great. He lived and reigned in the 7th century before Christ.

Cyrus II - called Cyrus the Great. He reigned from 559 B.C. until his death in 530 B.C. It is this Cyrus about whom we are writing.

Cyrus the Younger - the son of the Persian King Darius II.

As we have said before, our study will focus on Cyrus the Great. Let us begin our story with Astyages, the wicked grandfather of Cyrus.

Astyages was the last King of the Median Empire and reigned from 586 - 550 B.C. He had a terrifying dream that his daughter, Mandane, would give birth to a child who would rule all of Asia. Like Herod the Great, this wicked king did not want anyone to succeed him.

In an attempt to dilute his daughter's royal blood, he had her married to a Persian whom he deemed as inferior, and when her first child was born he ordered that the child be killed. This child would later be known as Cyrus the Great.

It is immediately obvious that the things which happened to this child did not happen by accident. God was determined to keep the baby alive that the Scriptures might be fulfilled, and the Devil was determined to kill the baby that the Scriptures might be broken.

The task of killing baby Cyrus was delegated to Harpagus, the king's most trusted servant. Harpagus, however, had second thoughts about killing the king's grandson. Since the king had no sons to succeed him, he reasoned that upon the death of Astyages, the sceptre would pass to his daughter, Mandane.

Once in power, he feared she would seek vengeance upon the man who had killed her son.

At last he determined that the baby had to die, but not by his hand. Thus, he delegated the task of killing the baby to a herdsman of the king named Mitradates. Mitradates was instructed to take the baby into the mountains and leave it to die.

The plot thickens . . . Mitradates was married to a female slave named 'Spaca," which incidentally means "bitch." This fact, as we will later point out, is quite significant. Spaca, not by accident, had just given birth to a stillborn baby boy.

The herdsman and his wife decided to exchange their dead baby for the live one. Thus, their dead son would have a royal burial and Spaca would not be deprived of the joys of motherhood by adopting the baby Cyrus.

Accordingly, Mitradates took the corpse of his own son into the mountains and exposed it. Three days later he presented that same corpse to Harpagus for burial.

The deception was not discovered for ten years, and its discovery grew out of an innocent game played by the village children. By "chance" the herdman's boy was chosen to play king. In the course of their game, he ordered that one of his disobedient subjects be whipped. Since the boy who was so punished came from a prominent family, the incident came to the attention of some important people. The herdsman's boy became the object of careful scrutiny and the herdsman was tortured on the rack until he told the whole story.

Harpagus, whom the king had originally commissioned to kill the child, was destined to pay a terrible price for his failure. He was invited to a sumptuous banquet and before him were placed the choicest morsels of boiled and roasted meat. At the end of the feast, he was presented a basket which contained the hands and the head of his own 13 year old son. It was only then that Harpagus realized that he had just dined upon the flesh of his own child. This fact too, was to be of critical importance in fulfilling the prophecy of God about Cyrus.

The wicked grandfather, still troubled about the dreams of his daughter's child, summoned his Magi. After much consultation, the Magi concluded that the king had nothing to fear from the boy Cyrus, for the fulfillment of the dreams, they said, had already been accomplished by the child's game. Thus, Cyrus was sent to Persia to be with his parents, who for the past ten years had believed him dead.

Now ancient peoples were much given to mythology. Rome, for example, was said to have been founded by Romulus and Remus, who were abandoned in the wilderness and were suckled by a she-wolf. Since the foster mother of Cyrus was named "Spaca" which means "bitch" the story soon was circulated that Cyrus, too, had been abandoned and raised by a bitch.

As Cyrus grew to manhood, his fame increased. Ultimately, Harpagus saw him as a vehicle through which he could gain vengeance over the king for the brutal murder of his son. Skillfully, he planted seeds of discord and rebellion in the minds of influential Medians. Ultimately, he sent a secret message to Cyrus which was sewn up inside the body of a dead rabbit. Cyrus, upon reading the details of the coup, fomented a rebellion in Persia and led an army to attack his grandfather, Astyages.

The wicked king, as if deprived of his senses, appointed Harpagus to be the commander of his army, not realizing that he was, in fact, the principle conspirator against him.

Astyages was defeated and was kept as a prisoner until the day of his death, and Cyrus became the supreme monarch of the Medes and the Persians. The remarkable and incredible prophecies of Scripture were in the course of being fulfilled.

Since Isaiah 45:1 mentions the conquest of nations, loosing the loins of kings, and opening the two leaved gates, the description of the conquest of Babylon by Cyrus will be of particular interest to you.

As Cyrus advanced toward Babylon, he came to the banks of a stream called "Gyndes" which empties into the Tigris. The stream was so swift and treacherous that one of the sacred white horses was drowned trying to swim across.

Cyrus was so enraged at the insolence of the river that he determined to break its strength so that a woman could walk across its waters without wetting her knees. Accordingly, he directed his army to dig 180 trenches on each side of the river, leading off in all directions. The water of the river thus diverted in 360 different channels was tamed, but not without the loss of an entire summer season. This "chance" incident, however, would play a critical role in the conquest of Babylon.

Having wreaked his vengeance upon the Gyndes, Cyrus set out the following spring for Babylon. A battle was fought some distance from the city, and the Babylonians were forced to retreat into the city.

The city of Babylon was felt to be virtually impregnable. Its towering rampart walls formed a perimeter 56 miles long around the city, and were 300 feet high and 90 feet thick. The River Euphrates flowed through the midst of the city, but was adequately protected by walls on each side of the river.

Cyrus, however, had recently discovered that the waters of a river could be tamed. He therefore, left part of his army where the Euphrates entered the city, and part of his army where it made its exit. He then took a third group of men upstream from the city and diverted the river waters into a marsh. The river thus became so shallow that it reached only midway up to a man's thighs.

This information is recorded by Herodotus in Herodotus 1:191, and I will here report the next part of the story in his own words:

> Had the Babylonians been apprised of what Cyrus was about, or had they noticed their danger, they would never have allowed the Persians to enter the city, but would have destroyed them utterly; for they would have made fast all the street gates which gave upon the river, and mounting upon the walls along both sides of the stream, would so have caught the enemy as it were in a trap. But, as it was, the Persians came upon them by surprise and so took the city . . .

Herodotus continues that the city of Babylon was involved in a festival of dancing and revelry. We read about it in the book of Daniel and the 5th chapter. During the midst of the banquet by Belshazzar, a sleeveless hand wrote his doom in unforgettable letters across the wall, and his kingdom was given into the hands of the Medes and the Persians.

Belshazzar was so frightened that his knees smote one against another (Dan. 5:6), and the two leaved gates which opened to the river were carelessly left open. The city of Babylon was captured and the Scriptures were remarkably fulfilled.

REFLECTIONS

Here we have a remarkable story. A part of it is found in the Bible, and a part of it is found in secular history. Each compliments the other, so that there is a beautiful harmony between them. There is no conflict between inspired truth and uninspired truth.

Even the most cautious and devout student of the Scriptures will, therefore, probably find this story interesting and intriguing, and perhaps even edifying.

We will place complete confidence in the Scriptural part of the story, and will hold to the rest as tentatively true, realizing that additional information may lead us at some later point in time to revise our position.

This is the way it should be! Extra biblical information should be judged by the Scriptures and not vice versa.

We shall now endeavor to proceed from a remarkable story that happened over 2,000 years ago . . . to remarkable stories that happen today. If these stories, or experiences, are contrary to the Scriptures, we must summarily reject them as wrong. The Scriptures have stood the test of time.

If these stories, however, are not contrary to the Scriptures, and if they enhance our service for God, I suggest that they may very well be valid contacts with the Christ . . . beyond the veil.

Our next chapter is entitled "Into the Deep" and contains some remarkable stories about answers to prayer. If you believe that God does not give wisdom to those who pray for it, you will find this next chapter quite offensive. If, on the other hand, you have longed for guidance and direction from God in your life today . . . you will find a certain exhilaration in seeing His hand at work in the lives of others.

35

THOUGHT QUESTIONS FOR CHAPTER II

1. Which is more true, inspired truth, or uninspired truth?
2. God had plans for Cyrus before he was born. Does God have plans for us before we are born?
3. List some of the ways in which the Devil tried to keep the prophecies about Cyrus from coming true.
4. List some of the providential things which happened to Cyrus which helped in fulfilling the prophecy.
5. Discuss the difference between "accident" and "providence."
6. Is it possible that spiritual forces are at war over us much as they were over Cyrus?
7. Have you ever had close calls when you were near death?
8. Is it possible that God has a special reason for sparing your life?
9. If God wanted to give you guidance today, how do you think He would do it?
10. How can we discern the leading of God from that of the Devil?

III

INTO THE DEEP

Launch out into the deep, and let down your nets for a draught (Luke 5:4).

It is not at all uncommon to go to a convention and hear the words, "This program will work . . . if you will work it." Frequently, however, our programs do not work and we go back to the next convention guilt ridden and embarrassed. If only we had worked harder . . . if only we had been more diligent . . . it surely would have worked.

What we sometimes say about a program could also be said about a fishing net. "This net will work if you will work it." Every time a fisherman casts a net, he has a statistical chance of catching fish. If he is a knowledgeable fisherman, his percentages of success will probably be better than those of a novice. But, sometimes even good nets do not seem to work.

The disciples of Jesus were fishermen by trade. They had spent their lives on the Sea of Galilee. They knew when to fish, and where to fish . . . yet they had fished all night and caught nothing.

At this point in time, the "Carpenter" told them to "launch out into the deep" for a draught.

They were extremely reluctant to do so. First of all, the night-time was the best time to fish, and it was now day. Secondly, the deep water was not the best place to fish. The shallow waters would enable them to gain the most efficient use of their net as there the weights and floats would enable them to completely trap their quarry. In the third place, a great crowd was watching and the advice to "launch out into the deep" had come from a carpenter. Finally, they had already toiled all night and taken nothing . . . their nets were washed and dried for storage . . . and they were totally exhausted.

Yet . . . at the word of Jesus, they let down their nets into the deep. . . . The catch of fish was so remarkable that it even tore their nets.

Let me suggest for your thinking that many of our present failures may not be the result of laziness and indifference. I am convinced that it is possible for us to labor all night long and still catch nothing.

Success comes when we are able to communicate with Christ!

TWO PREACHERS NAMED ROY

A number of years ago, Roy Stedman was working with a new congregation in Oceanside, California. He is a devout man who is much given to prayer. Therefore, before he began canvassing the community, he drove around praying for insight as to where he should begin.

God grants wisdom to those who ask for it . . . nothing doubting. The next day Roy parked his car and prayed that God would give him at least one good call that day.

At the third house on which he called, the lady responded: "Come right in Mr. Stedman, I just this moment got up from my knees in prayer asking God to send somebody to help me."

The skeptic will undoubtedly relegate such a story to coincidence. Brother Stedman did not think so . . . and neither do I.

Another preacher named Roy had a dramatic and similar answer to prayer. His name is Roy Weece. Roy first told me this story when he was ministering in Eldon, Missouri. He repeated it recently over KOBC, which is a 30,000 watt radio station in Joplin, Missouri. Here are notes adapted from that radio program:

Several years ago I became convinced on the basis of John 7:17 that God does give subjective evidence to the believer. This evidence will not contradict objective or revealed truth, nor will it precede our obedience to God. There must be obedience and trust in my life for this subjective evidence to occur.

Acts 8 was also intriguing to me. Philip, the Christian, was directed to the Ethiopian nobleman to tell him about Jesus and baptize him along the road. I figured that if God could lead people together in that day, I couldn't see any reason why He couldn't lead people together in this day.

So I decided to pray that God would guide me to people . . .

One example of this guidance came out west of Eldon, Missouri, in the vicinity of Versailles. I had been given the name of a man who lived in that vicinity. I had been told that he worked during the daytime and that I would have to catch him in the evening, but still I felt a strong compulsion to go down that road, and go into his yard. I had never been there before. I came up to his porch and knocked on the door and just about turned to walk away, for I just knew that he wouldn't be there.

Then the door opened, and there he stood. I introduced myself and said that I was a Christian and that I wanted to talk with him. He said, "Come right in." He took me over to a chair. On the chair was a gun. He said, "I was just seated on this chair with this gun to my temple. I had decided that life was not worth going on. Then I decided that before I did it I would try to call on God. And so I laid the gun aside, knelt down at this chair, and said, God, send somebody to help me."

It was at this point that Roy Weece knocked at the door! The man did not commit suicide, and ultimately gave himself to the Lord Jesus Christ and was baptized in a pond near his home.

Even though suicide is in epidemic proportions here in the United States, the statistical probability that you would arrive at someone's house at the very time they were in the act of blowing their brains out is quite remote. Roy Weece is convinced that somehow, God providentially directed him to that man's home at the precise moment when he was most needed. I share this conviction.

When Jesus called Peter, Andrew, James, and John to become fishers of men, He did so immediately following the miraculous draught of fish which these men had taken by launching out into the deep. Is it not possible that Jesus wanted to help these men catch other men with the same miraculous aid which enabled them to catch fish?

At the very time I am writing these words, my good friend, Gordon Clymer, opened the door to deliver some paper. Since he has an exciting story to share, I feel that his arrival at this time is providential.

Since Gordon is dictating this story to me now, I will record it in the first person:

> Ziden Nutt and I had gone to the Dominican Republic to discuss leadership training by means of a satellite network called "Project Lookup." We had been invited by Gordon Thompson, who had previously been a missionary to Puerto Rico, but was now working in the Dominican Republic.
>
> Since Ziden had successfully used a mobile unit to communicate the gospel in Africa, Brother Thompson expressed a strong interest in having such a unit for their work.
>
> He and his wife served as translators for teams of American eye doctors who came regularly to the Dominican Republic. They would go into the mountain villages and treat eye infections, fit glasses, and also treat other eye disorders.
>
> After the medical work was finished, the evenings were free for the missionaries to preach and to pass out Bibles and gospel tracts. The possibility of showing films would attract a large crowd, but the small mountain villages had no electricity. A

mobile unit, with its own generator, would provide an ideal solution to this missionary's need.

We had discussed this need all morning long, as well as the evening before. At noon, Brother Thompson received a telegram instructing him to call a supporting church in Oregon. Since he had no telephone at his residence, we went to a local hotel to make the call.

The reason for the call involved a late model International Travelall. Through the providence of God, this vehicle had been made available to the church and they were anxious to give it to the Thompsons if they had a need for it.

It was the ideal vehicle which he needed to have made into a mobil unit. That very day arrangements were made to send it to Joplin, Missouri, to the facilities of Good News Productions, International where it could be equipped with projectors, speakers, and all other necessary equipment. This vehicle, as far as I know, is still on the mission field accomplishing the very purpose that we were discussing that day.

In retrospect, it needs to be pointed out that at the time the church sent the telegram for Gordon Thompson to call, they had no concept of a mobile unit, and certainly had no way of knowing that he would at that very time be discussing such a need.

Also, we should observe that Gordon Thompson at that time had no idea that a supporting church would be given the very vehicle which he so desperately needed.

Thus, we have several facets to this amazing story. First of all, the missionary who had the need, secondly, the church which could supply that need, and finally, the man with the necessary technical experience and facilities to equip the vehicle. I believe it was God who orchestrated the entire matter, but it could not have happened if those who were involved had not responded to God's leading.

ALMOST IS BUT TO FAIL

Several years ago I was returning from a seminar with a van load of preachers. Our discussion fell to God's providential

41

guidance, and a fellow preacher, whom I regard as a close personal friend, related this story. Since the story does not have a happy ending, I will not mention his name.

This man was preaching in a community where a professional women's basketball team played a game. He attended that game, and returned home after the game was over. As he prepared for bed, he felt a strong compulsion to go back to the gymnasium and preach the gospel to those women.

After some reluctance, he put his clothes back on and questioning his own sanity, returned to the gymnasium. No one was there.

The preacher, however, knew the direction they would have to travel, so he started off in that direction. Soon he arrived at a junction and was no longer certain which direction to take. He determined to go just another mile or two, and if he did not see their bus, he would go back home where he belonged.

Within the parameters of his own conviction, he saw their bus at an all night cafe. Since it was now about midnight, these girls were virtually the only ones who were there. As he opened the door and walked in, they looked his way . . . almost as if they expected him to say something to them.

At this point, with some embarrassment, the preacher confessed that he had chickened out. The whole event had seemed so bizzare and his years of conventional training and conditioning prevented him from risking the irrational.

Like any "normal" person, the preacher offered them a casual greeting, sat down and ordered a cup of coffee . . . and then went home to bed.

This event had happened years before. It was the kind of thing you have to be careful about mentioning in some circles lest people label you as some sort of a nut. Nothing of this nature had ever happened to him since that time, but I think the next time it does, this brother will rise to the occasion. Almost is but to fail!

The apostles too, could have gone home to bed where they "belonged." They didn't have to risk the embarrassment of launching out into the deep. They could have played it safe and no one would have even known what would have happened otherwise.

But, praise God, they launched out into the deep. As irrational and embarrassing as it might have been, they rose to the occasion. Their lives were never the same. They dropped their fishing nets and followed Jesus to become fishers of men.

When you launch out into the deep and taste the victory of His miracle working power, you will never be the same again either.

The Scriptures command us to enter in boldly into the holiest of all by the blood of Jesus Christ, through the veil, that is to say, his flesh.

IT DOESN'T SOUND RIGHT

If I were to tell you that God was able to do all that you would ask, it wouldn't sound right . . . and it isn't.

If I were to tell you that God was able to do above all that you would ask, it wouldn't sound right . . . and it isn't.

If I were to tell you that God is able to do abundantly above all that you would ask, it wouldn't sound right . . . and it isn't.

If I were to tell you that God is able to do exceedingly abundantly above all that you would ask, it wouldn't sound right . . . and it isn't.

The Scriptures actually teach that God is "able to do exceeding abundantly above all that we ask or think, according to the power that worketh in us . . ." (Eph. 3:20).

The world's greatest power is not in man's ability to manipulate with levers . . . or to harness from nature . . . not even in the power of the atom. The greatest power in the universe is the power of God which created the atom and holds the universe together by His omnipotence.

This is the power that is available to you and to me . . . beyond the veil!

THOUGHT QUESTIONS FOR CHAPTER III

1. If you were Peter, why would you be reluctant to cast your nets into the deep?
2. Why are we sometimes reluctant today to "take a chance"?
3. Have you ever said a prayer without the slightest idea that God would answer that prayer? Why?
4. Which is more important, hard work or prayer?
5. Why did the early church set aside seven men to serve tables (Acts 6:2-4)?
6. What does it mean, "Whatsoever is not of faith is sin" (Rom. 14:23)?
7. Have you ever felt that you "ought" to do something which you failed to do?
8. How can God guide people who will not do what they feel they ought to do?
9. What has God done in your life in the last week?
10. What would you like for Him to do?

IV

FUELING A FLAME

Where no wood is, there the fire goeth out . . . (Prov. 26:20).

This principle is quite obvious. Where no wood is, the fire goes out.

The application of this principle in the proverb before us however, deals with the use of the tongue, and in particular, the negative use of the tongue. It is a Scripture against "talebearing" or "gossip."

The last half of the proverb concludes, ". . . so where there is no talebearer the strife ceaseth."

This is certainly true. Any minor problem contains a major potential for trouble if enough people talk about it in the wrong way.

James wrote about the use of the tongue and said, "Behold, how great a matter a little fire kindleth!" (James 3:5).

I was told of a congregation in southern Illinois that was building an educational unit. In the course of construction,

45

two Sunday School teachers had a heated dispute over the size of their respective classrooms. If no one had talked about that dispute, the fire would undoubtedly have gone out.

The dispute, however, became a major source of conversation in the community. The more they talked about it, the bigger was the fire. Ultimately, the congregation split and the building project was abandoned.

"Where no wood is, there the fire goeth out: and where there is no talebearer, the strife ceaseth."

I am convinced, however, that this Scripture has a positive application as well as a negative. What we talk about has a definite effect on our lives. The more we talk about generosity and generous people, the more apt we are to become generous. The more we talk about prayer and answers to prayer, the more likely we are to pray. The more we talk about evangelism and souls that are saved, the more likely we are to become evangelistic. Where no wood is the fire goeth out!

Since I desire to meet with the Lord within the veil, I am determined to talk about it. This will involve answers to prayer and the discussion of subjective experiences which I previously would have been embarrassed to discuss in public. Now I am convinced that the more I talk about these experiences, the more likely I am to have them.

The Psalmist wrote that God "inhabitest the praises of Israel" (Ps. 22:3). The more we praise Him, the more room we make for Him in our lives.

"POOF, I WAS WELL"

Some time ago I was invited by a group of missionaries to speak at a conference in central Brazil. In the course of the conference, a little boy got sick. His parents, Jim and Vanita Davis, are missionaries with many years of faithful service. They had given their sick child what medicine they had available, but several days had passed and he still had a fever and was nauseous. Finally, they came to the preachers and asked for prayer and the anointing of oil. Their request was based upon their understanding of James 5:14,

> Is any sick among you? Let him call for the elders of the church; and let them pray over him, anointing him with oil in the name of the Lord . . .

Not everybody shared the same understanding of this Scripture. Some preachers felt that this verse was only for those in the First Century. Others may have had some reservation or another about the manner in which the request was made or carried out.

Be that as it may, within a very short time after their request for prayer was honored, the little Davis boy was playing with his friends without any nausea or fever. He told Ruth Sanders (at that time a veteran of 35 years on the mission field in Brazil), "The men prayed for me, and poof, I was well!"

This is not intended to be a technical book of exegetical studies, it is a book on personal experiences. You could not go to court and "prove" that God healed this little boy. Perhaps the illness had run its course and he would have gotten well anyhow.

The little boy, however, felt that God had healed him, and I felt the same way. Even if I had not felt that way, I can see no real purpose in trying to convince the boy otherwise.

Furthermore, I want to fuel those fires that help my faith. So that evening in our meeting, I went out of my way to call attention to this little boy and to focus everyone's attention on what I believe was an answer to our prayer, and an experience which we might say was "beyond the veil." Where no wood is, the fire goeth out!

OXEN AND WATCHES

Deuteronomy 25:4 teaches, "Thou shalt not muzzle the ox when he treadeth out the corn." Paul quotes this passage in

I Corinthians 9:9 and insists that the real reason why God inspired those words involved people and not oxen. God was merely using oxen to teach a spiritual principle: that the laborer was worthy of his reward.

God can take little things of no real value and use them to teach us truths of eternal significance.

This principle came alive to me several years ago when I took my Sunday School class on a hike. There were nine young men there that day from ten to twelve years of age. They were overflowing with energy, and for the first half mile I had to run to keep up with them.

By the time we came to the creek, they were strung out over 50-75 feet.

We went up the creek for a quarter mile or so and paused at a little beach to throw stones into the water.

Next we struck out across a little meadow. Then we came to a draw that led through the woods up to a railroad track.

It was at this point that Scotty Helms announced that he had lost his watch.

I judge that we had already traveled a mile and a half, and maybe more. We had covered a variety of terrain ranging from overgrown trails to tall grass and deep leaves. During much of the hike, we had not gone in single file. It would be difficult to even retrace our steps exactly as we had taken them, let alone to find the lost watch.

"What do you think our chances are of finding the watch?" I asked. One young man responded "a hundred to one." Perhaps he was a bit optimistic.

Our dilemma was compounded by the fact that some of the boys had to be back at the church building in 35 minutes for Bible Bowl practice.

Does God care about watches? I really don't know, but I do know that He cares about little boys. Here was an opportunity to teach them something of eternal consequence.

First of all, I had the opportunity to teach them to care about someone who had a problem. Only one in our group had lost anything, but everybody in the group ought to share something of that loss with him.

Secondly, I had the opportunity to direct these young men to God, who is the ultimate solution to all of life's problems. We joined hands in a circle of prayer and I said, "God, you know exactly where the lost watch is, and I am asking you to help us find it."

Some 25 minutes later, Ralph Wakely found that watch, and my son, Paul, even found the little spring loaded pin that came out of the watch band causing it to fall from Scotty's wrist.

I gathered the boys for another circle of prayer. The watch was not of great value. At today's market a brand new watch just like it could be purchased for under ten dollars. The lesson we learned, however, is profoundly significant. God, who numbers the hairs of our head and watches every sparrow, longs to make our heart and mind the receptacle of His new covenant.

This was the kind of fire that I wanted to keep burning. We talked about it in Sunday School class. I told the story from the pulpit on Sunday. I wrote about the story in our church paper. Fires without fuel go out!

MEMOIRS OF ALEXANDER CAMPBELL

When I was in college many years ago, I studied a book called the *Memoirs of Alexander Campbell,* by Robert Richardson.

In that book, I read about some remarkable experiences which Mr. Campbell had that might be described as "beyond the veil." They were not experiences that grew directly out of a study of some passage of Scripture, but were personal experiences about which the Bible gave no direct instruction or advice. For many years, I glossed over these stories as inconsistent with the life of Mr. Campbell, whom I regarded as a careful student of the Scriptures. Now, I do not feel that his premonitions and answers to prayer are inconsistent at all, and I am determined to fuel this flame with the hope and prayer that I can receive similar insight and guidance.

For example, beginning on page 99 of Volume I is this remarkable story. It was October 7, 1808. The Campbells were in a ship riding at anchor and ready to sail to America. After family worship, Alexander fell into a somewhat uneasy slumber and presently awoke with evident marks of alarm. He told his mother and his sisters that he was confident of great and impending danger. In a most vivid dream, he thought that their ship had struck a rock causing water to come rushing in and nearly fill the vessel. He thought he had been making the most strenuous exertions to save the family and secure their luggage. Consequently, he said to his family,

> I will not undress to-night. I will lay my shoes within my reach, and be ready to rise at a moment's warning; and I would advise you all to be prepared for an emergency.

At about 10:00 that night, the winds veered toward the South and increased rapidly to a severe gale. In a few moments, the passengers were suddenly aroused by a violent shock, accompanied with the crashing sound of breaking timbers and the rushing of water into the main hold of the vessel.

Amidst the threat of capsizing the ship, the sailors and men with broad swords hewed down the masts which righted the vessel to some extent. The captain ordered the firing of minute-guns to signal their distress, but amidst the violence of the storm it seemed impossible that they could be heard on shore.

It was on this night that Alexander Campbell sat down upon the stump of a broken mast and dedicated himself to the Christian ministry. He thought of the many lessons he had learned from the Scriptures and his pious father, but more significant at that moment was the lesson that God communicates in the here and now. He was not just a God from history, but a God who was vitally involved in the present. In this conjunction Richardson says of Campbell,

He was a very firm believer in special providences, and was the more impressed on this occasion as, in his previous history, he had found his presentiments several times strangely verified. With him, these were simply facts which he did not pretend to explain upon natural principles, but regarded as indications of God's watchful care and interest in the affairs of his people (Vol. 1: p. 106).

It seems that Mr. Campbell also believed in experiences "Beyond the Veil" though he apparently did not use such terminology.

Another remarkable experience on Saturday, September 4, 1847, is recorded on page 556 of Volume II. The Campbells had lived in America since 1809, but in 1847 Alexander returned to the old world and in September of that year was lecturing in Glasgow, Scotland.

On the night of Saturday, September 4, Mr. Campbell was affected with a peculiar sadness for which he had no explanation. This was so entirely foreign to his nature that he could not avoid mentioning it the next morning at breakfast. Campbell's biography records his feelings with these words,

He felt as if some great calamity was impending, and he found it impossible to divert his mind from thoughts of home, which seemed to press upon him as never before . . . It is a singular circumstance that just about the time he experienced this unaccountable depression a sad affair was indeed occurring at his home across the Atlantic. On that very Saturday, his second and most beloved son Wickliffe, then in his eleventh year, was drowned. . . .

It needs to be observed that neither of these premonitions by Campbell is in conflict with any teaching of the Scriptures. The Devil certainly has power to perform supernatural signs and wonders and we must exercise great caution that we not be deceived by the wicked one.

In I Thessalonians 5:19-22 the Scriptures teach,

Quench not the Spirit. Despise not prophesyings. Prove all things; hold fast that which is good. Abstain from all appearance of evil. . . .

The Greek word used in "prove all things" is the word used for the assaying of metals. We are not to become gullible and irresponsible, but are commanded to scrutinize all things with the same diligence that an assayer has as he takes apart and analyzes samples of ore.

Campbell apparently examined these experiences and did not find them to be of the Devil. I'm not certain how much encouragement they gave to him . . . but I think they would have been of considerable encouragement to me. That's the reason I am so excited about talking about them.

JOE AND SANDY BARKER

Sandy Feathers Barker was a member of the youth group in Kingsport, Tennessee, when my good friend, Gordon Clymer, served there as associate minister. Her story, which was printed in the August 1980, issue of *Guideposts* was therefore of particular interest to us.

Joe and Sandy moved to Florida and went sailing for recreation. They ran aground on a sandbar and damaged the three foot stabilizer which served as a keel. Without this stabilizer, they were unable to steer and slipped sideways out into the open sea.

At this point, Joe threw out an anchor, but it tore loose from its cleat and disappeared. With no anchor, they hurriedly tried to lower the sail and in their haste knocked a fitting loose and lost the halyard which they would need to raise the sail again. The only way they could raise the sail again would be to lower the hinged mast to the deck and re-rig the line from its top. This would require a calm sea and no wind at all. The sea, however, was not calm.

Joe desperately fitted the oars into the oarlock and tried to row. It was hopeless. The high seas and the strong winds were tossing them like a toothpick in a torrent. Soon it was dark and the black waves pounded them so violently that they lashed themselves down with ropes to keep from being swept overboard.

The dawning of a new day did little to dispel their utter hopelessness and despair. At this juncture, Sandy looked down into the trusting eyes of their little dog and saw something profound and wonderful. The little dog had no fear because it trusted its master. She wondered why she did not trust God like her little dog had trusted her.

Somehow, she was emboldened to believe that God could calm the wind and the waves for them just as He had done for Jesus. So while the sun glowed low, they joined hands and prayed. Within five minutes, the six foot swells had melted into a sheet of still water. Sandy wrote that the experience was so awesome that she can still scarcely believe it.

The calm enabled them to accomplish a makeshift repair and again hoist the sail. Again they prayed, "Lord, we're ready, please give us wind to blow us back east to the shore." As if the Creator's hand was moving across the sea, a steady wind began to blow. It was blowing them in exactly the direction they needed to go so there was no need for steering. For twelve long hours they sailed until they fell asleep in utter exhaustion.

When they awoke, there was an erie calm. Their meager supply of water had long since been exhausted. Utterly helpless and vulnerable, they began to fear an impending storm. Sandy cried out again, "Oh, God, You've brought us this far, why have You left us here?"

The answer came soon. A 51 foot yacht loomed on the horizon. It was guided by very sophisticated electronic navigational equipment, yet "somehow" was 18 miles off course in just the right place to rescue Joe and Sandy Barker.

Within a few hours the storm hit with all its fury . . . but the Barkers were safe . . . and they had learned a lesson in trust which they would never forget. Not only did they not forget it . . . they were willing to share their praise in a public way. Praise the Lord! Where there is no wood the fire goes out!

LACKING WISDOM

A wise old preacher once asked a group of college students what the first requisite was for receiving wisdom from God. Some suggested "faith" and others said "asking." He then replied that the first requisite was to "lack wisdom."

Every parent has had the experience of trying to tell his children something . . . and not being able to. "I know daddy" they sometimes say. As long as they think they know the answer, it is very difficult to communicate with them. It is only when they hit bottom, so to speak, that they can be easily taught.

Focus all of your spiritual and mental energies on this beautiful promise from God:

> If any of you lack wisdom, let him ask of God, that giveth to all men liberally, and upbraideth not; and it shall be given him. But let him ask in faith, nothing wavering. For he that wavereth is like a wave of the sea driven with the wind and tossed. For let not that man think that he shall receive any thing of the Lord . . . (James 1:5-7).

There are some Christians who can truthfully say, "I have never received special wisdom from God." The Scriptures promise that some people will not receive anything from the Lord. Their arrogance, or perhaps their lack of faith, prevents them from claiming the promise and receiving the blessing.

I am "persuaded better things of you." The very fact that you have been willing to read this far in a little book about answers to prayer and providence is a strong indication that you have a desire to be close to God and that you have an openness to be instructed.

Therefore . . . GO FOR IT! Confess your ignorance and lack of wisdom. Pray about which man to marry . . . or which car to buy . . . or which job to take . . . or whatever other burden weighs heavily upon your heart today. And pray BELIEVING! God is all knowing. He has all the answers. He can deliver the godly out of temptation and reserve the unjust unto punishment.

When God answers your prayer . . . go public. Let your lips speak forth His praise. God will richly fill your life in such a circumstance for the Lord "inhabitest the praises of Israel."

And where there is no wood . . . the fire goes out!

THOUGHT QUESTIONS FOR CHAPTER IV

1. What did Jesus mean by, ". . . out of the abundance of the heart the mouth speaketh" (Matt. 12:34)?
2. Think of a time when gossip magnified an insignificant matter out of proportion.
3. Observe how not talking about that circumstance might have helped.
4. Why are some people reluctant to talk about answers to prayer?
5. What can be done to help people who have no answers to prayer?
6. Can Christianity be "caught" as well as "taught"?
7. What is the difference between wisdom and knowledge? Share a time when you received wisdom from God.
8. Who or what causes Christians to doubt God?
9. How is a double-minded person "unstable" in all his ways?
10. Think of special wisdom which you need right now and ask God in faith to receive it!

V

MONEY! MONEY! MONEY!

But thou shalt remember the Lord thy God: for it is he that giveth thee power to get wealth . . . (Deut. 8:18).

Have you ever dropped a fifty cent piece on a busy street corner, or in a crowded room. Somehow above the din of the traffic or the sound of human voices in animated conversation, the ring of cold cash has a special music to our ears.

If you really want to get somebody's attention—try money. The bigger the stakes, the more carefully we are apt to listen.

In this regard, I am personally convinced that God sometimes uses money as a means of getting our attention. Sometimes He lets us have money to get our attention; sometimes He takes money away from us to get our attention. My personal view of God is that He actually wants to get our attention and communicate with us. Frequently throughout the course of human history, He has condescended to communicate to man even

57

through the casting of lots or the putting out of various types of fleeces. Sometimes He jars us out of our complacency by means of money. Certainly, it is at least one way to get the average person's attention.

I remember with great appreciation to God an incident that occurred many years ago in a former ministry. A close personal friend had died of cancer and I had the privilege of conducting her funeral. No honorarium was given to me at the funeral and none was expected. We had been very close, and she was almost like a part of the family. I was honored to help in any way.

Some weeks later, her husband pressed something into my hand as he walked out of church services on Sunday morning. It turned out to be a check for $175. He had appreciated the trips which I had made to Kansas City to see his wife and wanted to show his appreciation by this gift. My initial reaction was to return the gift. But after comparing notes with my wife, I discovered that we had an immediate financial need of which I had not been previously aware. Since both of us had been writing checks on the same account with separate check books, we would be $174.25 overdrawn as soon as the checks just mailed cleared the bank.

I prayerfully swallowed my pride and thanked Jesus for supplying our need when I had not even been aware of it. I jokingly volunteered to return the 75¢ overpayment, but this offer was good naturedly declined.

Such an experience has a tendency to put a spring in my step and faith in my heart. It helps me not to worry about my daily bread and gives me the wonderful reassurance that my God can supply my every need. It was a brief contact with the supernatural that whets my appetite for something more . . . not something more of money . . . but something more of God.

HARVEY BACUS

Harvey Bacus is the head of the Missions Department of a Christian college in Joplin, Missouri. Harvey was on the mission field before coming to the college and has a treasure chest of many stories about the providential working of God "beyond the veil."

For example, he said that one day a generous brother walked into his office with $2,000 to give to missions. He requested only that he be allowed to remain anonymous. He had just walked out the door and was not 20 steps away when Chris DeWelt hurried in the room with an urgent need for $1,000. Chris had been downstairs in the missions building talking to missionaries in Chile by ham radio. Chris was instructed that the money had to be in the bank by closing time and that he was to borrow the money if he was able to. It was not necessary for Chris to borrow the money, for God had already made provision for that need before he had even asked.

Within an hour after Harvey received the money, another urgent appeal came to the office for $1,000 which was needed to help a missionary get to Taiwan. The mission trip was not delayed. Thank you Jesus! God had foreseen the need for these two $1,000 expenditures and prompted a precious member of His Spiritual Body to supply that need. The reason why that brother knew to give the $2,000 is "beyond the veil" and you have to be there yourself before you can ever understand.

Our God owns all the beasts of the forest and even the cattle upon a thousand hills. He does not need our money to survive. We, however, are in desperate need of Him. He is rich beyond our wildest imagination and encourages us to "ask" that we might receive.

DR. GARLAND BARE

Dr. Garland Bare was born on the Thai-Tibetan border to heroic missionary parents. Their ventures in faith would fill many volumes and yet not be able to tell the whole wonderful story of God's working in their lives. Permit me therefore, to narrow our vision and focus only on a few brief incidents "beyond the veil."

When Garland and his wife prepared to go to the mission field, they made the same vow that Hudson Taylor and George Muller had made many years before. They determined that they would never ask men for money or support. This was not intended to impune the motives or the mission of others who do, it was only the response of their own hearts to a personal conviction about the way that God was leading them personally.

Down through the years of their mission work, God has never failed to supply their every need, and has frequently supplied far beyond what they had even imagined He would do.

Garland was 33 years old when he felt led of God to become a medical doctor. He had begged and pleaded for years in a vain attempt to get a doctor to come to his remote area of the jungle, and at last concluded that God might be leading him to answer his own prayers.

There were at least four gigantic obstacles which made this dream seem impossible. First of all, Garland Bare was not a Thai citizen. There were only 60 openings available at the medical school and there were 25 qualified Thai citizens available for every opening. In the second place, Brother Bare was married. At that time in Thailand, no person was allowed to go to college who was married, and if you got married after beginning your schooling, you would be expelled. In the third place, no person over 25 years of age was being allowed in the program and Garland was 33 at the time. Finally, Brother Bare had no pre-med schooling and had been out of school for 13 years.

Our God, however, is a God of miracles who specializes in the impossible. The Scriptures teach that He not only gives us a desire to do something for Him, but He also gives us the ability. This is my understanding of Philippians 2:13, "For it is God which worketh in you both to will and to do of his good pleasure." Thus, when God gave Garland Bare the desire to be a medical doctor, He also gave him the ability. Now it was up to him to work out his own salvation with fear and trembling. The Thai government waived all of their requisites and agreed to enroll him in med-school if he could accomplish all of his pre-medical schooling in only one year.

Garland Bare arrived in the United States for one year of pre-medical training. His trial class in chemistry was sucessfully completed in a manner which borders on the miraculous, and he was ready to enroll for the fall semester with only $15 in his pocket. The problem was that the initial payment for fall tuition was $50. Having nowhere else to turn because of his prior commitment, he turned to God in prayer. It was Tuesday, and he needed the necessary $50 by Friday.

At this point, Brother Bare felt a strong inclination to give away part of his precious $15. Another missions student was having financial difficulties and was planning to drop out of school. As irrational as it seems, Brother Bare put $10 in an envelope with a note of encouragement and slipped it under the student's door. He then returned to his own room feeling very much like he needed to see a psychiatrist.

The next morning, however, he went to the mailbox and found a $20 gift had arrived from a total stranger. Praise the Lord! He had doubled the gift he had given away and now had $25 of the $50 which he so desperately needed. It was now Wednesday, and he had only two days left.

On Thursday another check arrived in the mail. Sometime before, Garland had done some work for the American Bible Society and a check for $50 was now received in payment for those services. Now his prayers had been answered and he had the money for which he had prayed, and even more.

Those who are led of the Spirit sometimes do things which seem irrational to others. At this point Brother Bare said,

> Would you believe it, that something came up that day, a very urgent need of another Christian, and I gave that $50 to that person?

With only a few hours left before the deadline, however, another check arrived from a fellow missionary to Thailand

61

for $150. With the first gift Brother Bare had received twice as much in return, and with this gift he had received three times as much.

Garland Bare, however, was not trying to double or triple his money, he was trying to follow the leading of the indwelling Christ. He was "beyond the veil" in a personal encounter with the Lord and was following the leading of those impulses from the Holy Spirit.

Certainly, experiences like this would cause even the most hardened skeptic to scratch his head and wonder.

Upon another occasion, Garland and his wife had an urgent need for 1,500 baht in Thai currency. At the time, this was only about $75 in American currency. Again they prayed, but no funds came. Finally, they determined that they would have to borrow the money. Sixteen kilometers away was a Chinese merchant who had loaned them money before and thus Brother Bare wrote a letter containing his request. He placed the letter on the bookshelf ready to send it the next morning.

Early the next morning, however, the Chinese merchant himself showed up on a bicycle. It was raining. He said, "Do you need 1,500 baht?" "Why, yes," replied Brother Bare, "how did you know?" "I had the strongest feeling" he said, "It was almost like a dream." Then he handed over the 1,500 baht and walked away saying, "You sure do serve a powerful God!" The letter had never even been mailed.

Yes, we do serve a powerful God. He is constantly teaching us to "ask" that we might receive. If we who are evil know how to give good things unto our children, how much more shall our Father which is in heaven give good things unto those that ask Him!

DAVID CORTS

Here is another story about a preacher and money. His name is David Corts.

David Corts was ordained to the ministry in September 1960. By his own testimony, he originally had no desire to be a preacher of the Gospel. With some reluctance, he agreed to spend one year in a Christian college, but he was determined not to be a preacher. He had a sister that was married to a preacher, an older brother that was a preacher, a next older brother that was a preacher, and he was absolutely certain that he would never be a preacher. It was only out of a sense of reverence for what he knew his parents were praying for, that he agreed to go to a Christian college at all.

After several months under Biblical teaching, he began to waver a little. He still, however, was avoiding any kind of Christian service or commitment that would tie him down to the ministry.

At this juncture, he received a notice from the college that he would have to pay up his bill in the cafeteria or he would not be permitted to continue in school. David came from a large family with seven children . . . yet he knew he could write home and get help. The letter from the college, however, seemed to be a convenient way to avoid being a preacher.

David said that it was on a Friday in the month of March, and his bill had to be paid by the following Monday. He got down on his knees and placed the letter on the bed where the Lord could read it. At this point he made a "deal" with the Lord. In retrospect, he knows you are not supposed to make "deals" with the Lord, but that's what he did anyhow. He said,

> Lord, if you want me to be a preacher, then this will be taken care of, and if you don't want me to be a preacher then it won't be taken care of—then I'll know for sure!

When he arose from his prayer, he felt terrific. He was confident that the bill would not be taken care of . . . and he would not have to be a preacher.

In Saturday morning's mail, however, was a letter from a woman named Ada Richman. He couldn't even remember who

Ada Richman was. She was not a member of the same church that he was . . . and he had only met her on one occasion . . . and that meeting had been quite casual.

The letter read,

Dear David, I've been thinking of you all week long and the only thing I can think of is that you need money.

In the letter was much more than enough money to cover his bill.

Ada Richman has now gone to be with Jesus, but David, who did enter the Christian ministry, and who is at the time of this writing preaching in one of the biggest Christian churches in America, told her that every soul he wins to Christ, she has an investment in.

Is it not possible that this is another beautiful experience "beyond the veil" to fill a young man's life with guidance and help as he began his commitment to preach the Gospel.

JANET WILSON

Janet Wilson, speaking to the 1986 Women's Convention in Joplin, Missouri, shared a series of inspirational stories which reflect her unswerving commitment to Christ and remarkable answers to prayer.

Early in her Christian life, she learned the power of "calling things which be not as though they were" (Rom. 4:17). After many frustrating attempts to win her mother to Christ, she released her to Jesus and began to praise Him for her salvation . . . even before it came to pass. Her mother was baptized into Christ just six short months before passing into eternity. Praise the Lord!

Since a recent answer to prayer involved money, we include it here with the hope and prayer that it will provide help and inspiration to you who are beset by financial problems.

Janet was working with her son in starting a new work in Townhead, Jamaica. So many people were coming to Christ that the house where they were meeting would not hold them all and they purchased a tent. Janet prayerfully contacted her friends and supporters and raised the $3,000 for the tent . . . only to discover that she needed $9,000 more to purchase land.

They had assumed that they would be able to rent or lease land . . . but they were wrong. The only land appropriate for their need in the area they were working belonged to a man named Mr. Gordon. He wanted $30,000 Jamaican money for the property and would not come down in the price or sell only part of the land.

With some reluctance, Janet again contacted her friends and supporters for additional funds. She had three months to raise the money . . . but failed. Based on an exchange rate of 3.4 to 1, she calculated that it would take approximately $9,000 American money to equal $30,000 in Jamaican currency. All she could raise, however, was $6,000.

Instructing the believers to pray, Janet and Ed Thomas went to the bank believing that God would not allow the gates of hell to prevail against His church. Would you believe it? On that day the exchange rate was not 3.4 to 1, but 5 to 1. The $6,000 which God had enabled her to receive was the precise amount needed on that day to purchase the land.

Janet said that she began to shout for joy and wondered if any of the women from America had heard her. She was "beyond the veil," but was crying out for the rest of us to come on in and enjoy the view.

FROM RAGS TO RICHES

One of the most unusual "Cinderella stories" I have ever been personally associated with is the story of Sam and Katie Butcher. I have been privileged to go over this story with them on the radio and also on video tape.

The video interview is available through Good News Productions International, in Joplin, Missouri.

65

Sam and Katie had poverty with a capital "P." For the first seven years of their marriage, they did not have enough money to even own an automobile.

At a time when they had five children, they sometimes had nothing to eat but oatmeal. Katie says that they would place a sheet upon the floor and sprinkle raw oatmeal upon it. Then pretending that they were receiving manna from heaven, they would eat . . . and somehow be satisfied.

Upon one occasion, however, she said they did not even have oatmeal . . . they had nothing. They sat down at the table and gave thanks anyhow. Then they went for a walk and sang praises to God. Katie said it was a beautiful time of the year and the apple trees were in blossom.

When they returned . . . there was food upon the table . . . A friend who was moving knew of their need and had brought by some perishable goods from his refrigerator and other things which he didn't want to move. Since there was no one home, he came on in and left the food on the table.

Out of this abject poverty, Sam and Katie Butcher became multi-millionaires in only three short years. They are internationally famous for the "Precious Moments" ministry which they believe has been given to them by God. Sam says that Precious Moments figurines are the number one collectible in the United States.

It is impossible to understand their ministry without a recognition of their belief in a personal relationship with Jesus Christ and answers to prayer in the here and now.

Typical of their life-style is the manner in which they felt led of God to move to Carthage, Missouri.

They began to feel that God was leading them to move from Michigan. Therefore, Sam elected to drive home from a business trip to California, in a rented car. Periodically, he would call his wife in Michigan and pray about locations. She had a large map upon the wall and would mark his presence with pins as they prayed.

Sam said that once in New Mexico, he drove back some 10 miles to a town he had just passed through. He felt certain that this was not the place where they should live, but wondered why he felt the urge to return.

Spying an old Indian Mission, he thought that God might have wanted him to help them financially . . . and wrote out a check. After taking a tour of the facility, he asked his guide what it would cost to fix up the place . . . it was the exact amount of the check which he had already made out.

Arriving in Joplin, Missouri, he got a motel and also a strong conviction that this was the place where God wanted him to move. He went to a real estate office and drew on his sketch pad a house which he had only seen with eyes of faith. It was an older house overlooking a little river with a smaller house below.

Sam was dressed in jeans with a tear on the knee and the first realtor thought he must be a brick or two short of a full load. Another older man, however, recognized the house as being just like one south of Carthage. Sam and Katie now live there . . . it is only a mile or so from the place where my eldest son and his family live. They are building a Precious Moments Chapel there which will undoubtedly be visited by people from all over America, and perhaps all over the world.

ALL KINDS OF EVIL

The Scriptures teach that the love of money is the root of all kinds of evil. Those who thirst for earthly wealth fall into temptations and snares and many foolish and hurtful lusts which drown men in destruction and perdition.

Everyone who serves God faithfully does not become rich. Millions of faithful Christians in third world countries and behind the Iron and Bamboo Curtains can testify to that. God may demonstrate His power in your life by keeping you poor. He may feed you with scavengers like Elijah who was fed by the lowly ravens. You may wind up like the proverbial widow who could always scrape the bottom of the barrel . . . but was never quite out. God can teach us of His presence in the absence of money as well as in its abundance.

As you consider your finances, however, please remember that it is an area of such interest to the human mind that God has frequently chosen to manifest His presence and concern through money.

May you enter in boldly into the Holiest by the blood of Jesus Christ. May God reveal treasures to you which moth and rust do not corrupt and which thieves do not break through and steal.

THOUGHT QUESTIONS FOR CHAPTER V

1. The Scriptures teach that Christians are to be satisfied with two things. What are they? (I Tim. 6:8)
2. Why do we sometimes find it difficult to be content without things which we really don't need?
3. How much money does it take to make you rich?
4. Paul was hungry and in need (I Cor. 4:11ff.). Was this an indication that he lacked in faith?
5. If someone gave you a million dollars, what would you do with it?
6. How does this compare with the way you spent your income last year?
7. Why would a loving father not give unlimited amounts of money to some children?
8. Name some things which you enjoy in Christ which moth and rust cannot corrupt and thieves cannot break through and steal.
9. Is it wrong to ask God for money?
10. Is it wrong for a Christian to be a millionaire?

VI

FOR SUCH A TIME AS THIS

. . . And who knoweth whether thou art come to the kingdom for such a time as this . . . ? (Esther 4:14).

ELIJAH

The Bible contains many miracles of timing. The components of the story, in and of themselves, may not be miraculous. It is timing, however, which frequently sets these events apart in our minds as experiences "beyond the veil." The fact that it did not rain in Israel for three years, for example, is not in and of itself miraculous. Many nations experience severe and prolonged drought. The fact that the drought began and ended, however, just when Elijah said that it would, does give us pause for some serious reflection (I Kings 17:1—18:46). James 5:17-18 encourages us to pray with the reminder that Elijah was a fallible human being just as we are.

69

ESTHER

Miracles of timing are particularly evident when reading the book of Esther. Wicked Hamaan had ordered the death of all Jewish people. This terrible edict was to be carried out on the 13th day of the 12th month, which is the month Adar. The Jews responded with fasting and prayer.

As a result of those prayers, a number of unusual things began to happen. At just the right time the king could not sleep. In the absence of sleep he called for the book of records and chronicles to be read before him and the passage selected just happened to be the right passage. Two of the king's chamberlains had plotted to kill the king, and a man named Mordecai just happened to be there at the right time to overhear their sinister conversation. Mordecai thus saved the king's life and under normal circumstances would have been immediately rewarded, but from God's perspective, the timing was not right.

In retrospect, we see that God waited until it was just the right time for the king, just the right time for Mordecai, just the right time for Esther, just the right time for the Jews, and just the wrong time for Hamaan and the Devil. The whole story was orchestrated by God like a precision clock so that the Jewish people were spared and wicked Hamaan was hanged upon his own gallows.

In the midst of this exciting drama, Mordecai asks Esther this piercing question, "and who knoweth whether thou art come to the kingdom for such a time as this?"

Esther just happened to be at the right place, at the right time. If she failed in her responsibility, God would have to bring about deliverance from another place, but she did not fail! She became the queen at just the right time, she petitioned the king at just the right time, she exposed the wicked Hamaan at just the right time, and none of these incidents of timing were accidental.

JESUS

The Scriptures teach that Jesus was born in the "fulness of time" (Gal. 4:4). Just as a woman's body becomes perfectly

70

prepared for the moment of birth, so also the world was ripe for the birth of Jesus. Individuals and empires were used by God to create the perfect atmosphere for the advent of the Messiah. The appearance of the angels, the decree of Caesar, the journey to Bethlehem, the visit from the wise men, the flight into Egypt, the murder of the infants, and countless other events were woven by our Omnipotent God into what is unquestionably the Greatest Story Ever Told. Each participant appeared on cue and performed as expected though few, if any, were fully aware of the part they were playing in the destiny of mankind.

PHILIP

When Philip the evangelist left his prosperous ministry in Samaria to go to a deserted roadway between Jerusalem and Gaza, it seemed both unfortunate and irrational. There appeared on that road, however, at just the right time, a eunuch of great authority from Ethiopia. He just happened to be reading from the scroll of Isaiah the prophet and as he drew near to Philip he just happened to be reading that beautiful and profound prediction about Jesus that He would be "led as a sheep to the slaughter . . ." Touche! The timing was perfect. Philip began at that Scripture and preached unto him Jesus. They came to a certain water and the eunuch was baptized into Christ and then went on his way rejoicing.

SPECTATOR OR PARTICIPANT

At this point in time, I am concerned that you, the reader, may have the mistaken idea that such miracles of timing could never happen to you. Unfortunately, the vast majority of people within the framework of Christendom have the mentality of spectators. We watch parades, we watch athletic events, we watch television, we watch the choir, we watch the preacher,

71

and our whole frame of reference is from the perspective of only a spectator.

One famous football coach has observed the irony of 22 men on the playing field who are in desperate need of rest, and 22,000 people in the grandstands who are in desperate need of exercise.

The need of the hour is for you to become a "doer" of the word and not just a "hearer." The Scriptures teach that those who only hear the word of God are guilty of a kind of self-deception. It is like looking in a mirror and then forgetting what manner of person you saw. It is living in a dream world without reality.

If you could have a personal experience "beyond the veil" it would transform your day from a dead experience with drudgery, into a thrilling adventure with an ever present power.

ANDY LAY

Some years ago Andy Lay was ministering with a congregation in Joplin, Missouri. Being caught between insurance policies, he found himself deeply in debt for medical expenses which he was unable to pay.

As the deadline approached and it became inescapably obvious that he had more bills than money, he began to blame God for placing him in that predicament. At the point of utter desperation, he was pacing the floor in the foyer of their church building. He glanced at the glass door just in time to see a sparrow fly into the glass and fall upon the sidewalk.

At this moment, Andy was reminded of the Scripture which teaches that not even a sparrow can fall to the ground without our heavenly Father's knowledge. Jesus, therefore, encourages us not to worry for we are of more value than many sparrows.

Deeply ashamed of his attitude, Andy repented of his rebellion at just the time the mailman walked up from the street. In the mail was an anonymous cash gift which was precisely the amount needed to pay all of his bills which were due.

In retrospect, Andy observed, that the timing of these incidents was the most remarkable aspect of their occurrence. He was at the lowest point of his desperation when God sacrificed the sparrow as a reminder of His care, and it was at the moment of his repentance that God sent the postman with the anonymous gift which he so desperately needed.

Is it not exciting to consider the possibility that God allowed that sparrow to come into being for such a time as this? All of the days of his life may have been orchestrated by God so that he could appear in one man's life at the precise moment when an encounter with Deity was most desperately needed.

Obviously, the money had been mailed some days before. Again, however, the thought was planted in someone's mind at precisely the right moment. The envelope was sealed and placed in the mailbox on just the right day. The postman arrived at the right address, with the right amount of money, at just the right time.

Great is the Lord and greatly to be praised. His providence was reserved for such a time as this!

MARJORIE HOLMES

Guideposts magazine contains an amazing story about Marjorie Holmes. On January 1, 1981, she was reflecting upon 47 years of happiness in marriage, and the sadness which she felt over the recent death of her husband. Enough time had lapsed that she was thinking about the possibility of remarriage and she prayed, "Please, God, send me a wonderful man who will love me and whom I can love." She was even bold enough to write down criteria which would characterize the man for whom she prayed. First upon the list was that he be "a believer, devout . . ."

On the same night, and at essentially the same time, a medical doctor named George Schmieler sat in his bedroom in deep despair. He was alone and bitter. His wife of 48 years had just passed away. She had not only been his wife, but also his secretary, bookkeeper, and nurse.

73

Dr. Schmieler was frustrated and bitter and began to blame God. At precisely that moment, his picture fell to the floor from his wife's dresser. There was no wind . . . no bolt of lightning . . . but the crash of the picture caused him to fall to his knees and ask help from God.

As he raised his head, he found himself staring at the closet door. For the first time, he noticed that the panels on that door formed a cross. Impulsively, he went to the closet where he found a book by Marjorie Holmes entitled, *I've Got to Talk to Somebody, God.*

The fact that Dr. George Schmieler and Marjorie Holmes became husband and wife gives us something to think about. Marjorie feels that for the believer there are no "coincidences" only "Godincidences." She and her future mate, whom she had never met before, lived many miles apart and it took a series of "Godincidences" to make them husband and wife.

As a matter of fact, it was not until their honeymoon that Marjorie found her list of requisites for a husband, and that she and George were able to compare notes and realize in retrospect that God had orchestrated and directed their entire courtship.

God had arranged their marriage for just such a time as this!

PERSONAL TESTIMONIES

Down through the years I have had a number of unusual experiences with reference to timing which I attribute to the remarkable power of God.

In 1974, I set out to visit a number of congregations to do research for a book. I was accompanied by my eldest son, John, and the late Mike Pratt.

When we arrived at San Jose, California, there were several that I had hoped to see. Among them was my old friend, Marvin Rickard, who ministers to the Christian Church in Los Gatos, just a few miles away. The congregation had grown to several thousand, and I was told that even members of his own church had to schedule appointments several weeks in advance.

We were picked up at the airport by Harold and Phyllis Lass and spent a leisure couple of hours catching up on old times. About 7:30 or so we went out to eat and without any particular place in mind, wound up at a large restaurant on South First Street. Since the parking lot was about full we had to park some distance from the door.

When we arrived at the canopy in front of the door, I was pleased to discover less than ten feet away, Marvin Rickard, who had just stopped his car to let out his wife. We ate together and enjoyed a beautiful fellowship which a few moments either way would have made impossible.

Consider the unusual "coincidences" involved in our meeting. Marvin had no idea that I was anywhere in the area or that I had hoped to see him. He merely took his wife out for a meal. Since the Bay Area of California has millions of people and thousands of restaurants, the statistical possibility that we would meet by chance is virtually non-existent. Had either of us arrived a minute earlier or later there would have been a good possibility that we could have eaten at the same restaurant and not even known of each others presence.

God's timing, however, is perfect.

Or consider the phone call which I received from Gerald Marvel. Brother Marvel preaches in Vancouver, Washington. To the best of my knowledge, we had never spoken to one another before.

Gerald and I both attended the same high school and graduated the same year. It was a large school, however, and we were not close friends. I had heard his name, and he had heard mine, but again, to the best of my knowledge, we had never spoken to one another before.

Sometime after graduation he attended a family reunion and his aunt informed him that Boyce Mouton had married Betty Coppenger and become a preacher.

His initial response was, "No! You've got the wrong guy." His aunt, however, assured him that it was so and asked him to give me a call. He promised that he would.

Since both of us had moved away, he had no idea where I was, but one day determined to honor his promise and give me a call. After several long distance calls, he found my parents, then my wife, and finally spoke for an hour or so long distance with me.

He then visited our home on his way back to Washington from a meeting in Texas.

From my own personal standpoint, his phone call and his visit could not have come at a more opportune time. I had been in a state of depression and indecision, and his ministry to me was more meaningful than words can describe.

The "rest of the story," so to speak, was that his aunt, to whom he had made his promise, had been dead for over 10 years when he remembered his promise and decided to call.

Again, this is more than a coincidence to me. God's timing is perfect. The seed had been planted ten years before it blossomed to bring fragrance into my life . . . but it arrived on schedule just the same.

QUITT'N NOTHING

Bob Cox tells of old fashioned "quitt'n meetings" down in Texas. Periodically, a spirit of repentance comes upon the church and they gather to testify about the things they intend to quit. Some are going to quit smoking, cussing, drinking, etc.

One little old lady moved to the platform. She was blessed with an impeccable record in the community and no one could imagine anything which she would have to quit. She stood on her tiptoes and peered over the pulpit to announce, "I ain't been doing nuthin' and I'm gonna quit it!"

Perhaps she speaks for a lot of us. We cannot go back and undo our yesterdays . . . and we cannot count upon tomorrows.

Now is the acceptable hour. Today is the day of salvation. When God places an impulse in your mind, it just may be that He is calling you to do His will . . . for such a time as this!

THOUGHT QUESTIONS FOR CHAPTER VI

1. Jesus knew that Judas would betray Him and also when he would do it. Does this mean that Judas did not have "free will" to make his own decisions?
2. Do we have "free will" to do anything today we want to do?
3. How can God guide people who have free will?
4. How does the Devil get people to do his will?
5. How can we tell whether an idea came from God or the Devil?
6. If God wanted you to send some money to someone today . . . how would He get you to do it?
7. Did Jesus ever get in a hurry?
8. What would have happened to the people of God if Esther had failed?
9. If God wanted you to make a call on someone today . . . how would He get you to do it?
10. Whom do the Scriptures liken unto a person looking in the mirror and forgetting what he sees (James 1:22-25)?

VII

FILLED WITH THE SPIRIT

And be not drunk with wine, wherein is excess; but be filled with the Spirit (Eph. 5:18).

A person who is drunk with wine is said to be "under the influence." They do not behave in an ordinary way. They are really not "themselves." They act differently. They walk differently. They talk differently. They are "under the influence" of bottled spirits.

We are not to be drunk with wine, but we are commanded to be "filled with the Spirit." Under the influence of the Holy Spirit, we also assume a new personality. We are not "ourselves" any longer. We act differently. We walk differently. And we talk differently. We are "under the influence," not of bottled spirits, but of the Holy Spirit. Or to use the vocabulary of Scripture, we are "filled with the Spirit."

At this point I must resist the temptation to become theological and to state my own personal views on various Scriptures. This, I fear, would become a merry-go-round of dispute which might take your eyes off of Christ and rob you of the personal joy of entering in boldly into the holiest of all. Beyond the veil is that profound "filling" of the Spirit which enables mortal men like you and me to do exceeding abundantly above all that we can ask or think by means of that new power operating within us (Eph. 3:17-20).

While many in the Christian world find the Holy Spirit a major subject for debate and dispute, there are others who find the Holy Spirit a major source of strength and power.

W. CARL KETCHERSIDE

W. Carl Ketcherside was born in abject poverty in a crude miner's cabin on May 10, 1908.

He was an exceptionally gifted child and when he entered the first grade he was advanced to the second in only two weeks, the third by Christmas, and was in the fourth grade by the end of the school year. At one point he averaged reading a book a day for a period of seven years.

For more than forty years, Brother Ketcherside was a leader in one of the most narrow and factional groups in Christendom. He frequently engaged in public debates with other Christian leaders. Now he describes his former ministry as that of a "piece" maker instead of a "peace" maker.

A dramatic change, however, came over him in 1951, while preaching in Belfast, North Ireland. In that divided and strife torn part of the world he saw his bigoted and divisive mentality in a new light. One night he knelt alone on the cold floor of an unheated church house. A deep snow was on the ground outside. For more than an hour he wrestled with his own conscience while the persistent Christ continued to knock at the door of his heart.

Over and over the Scripture came to mind, "behold I stand at the door and knock." Carl said that this had been one of his favorite Scriptures and he would speak on this subject on the last night of his gospel meetings. It now dawned upon him that these words were not spoken by Jesus to an alien sinner, but to lukewarm Christians.

At last, in desperation, he opened his heart to Jesus in a new and living way. Carl testifies that Jesus Christ did just exactly what He said He would do. He arose from his knees a new man. From that day until this, he has promoted love and unity in the body of Christ.

At the time of this writing he is in his late 70's and is pioneering a new work among the poor in the inner city of St. Louis.

The Scriptures teach, "Brethren, if a man be overtaken in a fault, ye which are spiritual, restore such an one in the spirit of meekness . . ." (Gal. 6:1).

This is precisely what W. Carl Ketcherside is doing. I personally see him as a man who is "filled with the Spirit," allowing the personality of Christ to progressively dominate his life with power and love.

JACOB AND ISRAEL

Students of the Scripture will recognize that Jacob and Israel were both names for the same man.

Jacob is an uncomplimentary name which means "heel catcher." He was so named because his hand was on the heel of his twin brother at the time of their birth (Gen. 25:26). Throughout the first part of his life, he was always conniving to trip up his brother and to manipulate men like a wrestler seeking to gain an advantage over an opponent.

How aptly this describes many Christians, always trusting in themselves, or their hard work, or their cleverness. Such manifest a form of godliness but have no power.

81

Jacob went through a cleansing process in the land of Padan Aram. His father-in-law, Laban, deceived and tricked him and changed his wages ten times. This was undoubtedly a part of the maturing process which transformed Jacob, the heel catcher, into Israel which literally means the "Prince of God."

The new name was given to him at Peniel, where he learned to have power with God. Now instead of trying to manipulate men, Jacob had learned to prevail with God, hence he was hereafter known as "Israel." Hosea makes reference to this contrast by writing,

> He took his brother by the heel in the womb, and by his strength (or in his manhood) he had power with God (Hos. 12:3).

BOB MOOREHEAD

Bob Moorehead had just such an experience as this in 1969, when he was ministering in Enid, Oklahoma. His ministry was going well on the surface, but his personal life was in a state of crisis. Not only was he ready to throw in the towel with reference to preaching, but even with regard to the Christian life itself.

He now considers his ministry to have been "in the flesh," and the 17 hour days had finally taken their toll. He was burnt out, withered, and shriveled.

In desperation he sought for the reality of God. Words do not do justice to the traumatic struggle which a man goes through in his own personal Peniel, but Bob Moorehead testifies that he came out of that experience a different man. He did not hear any voices, see any visions, or speak with other tongues, but he believes he was "filled with the Spirit." It was a turning point in his life and his ministry. Everything changed: his marriage, his preaching, his relationship with his wife and children . . . He states that his hunger for the Word of God went from "0 to 1000."

Bob is quick to point out that he was already saved . . . and that as such he possessed the indwelling Spirit of God. Perhaps this is the difference. In the first place he had the Spirit, and in the second the Spirit had him.

Not long after this life changing encounter with Deity, Bob felt led of God to leave his church in Oklahoma, and serve a little congregation in Kirkland, Washington. The church in Washington was only about one tenth the size of the church in Oklahoma. Naturally the salary would be smaller too . . . and the living expenses would be higher. Oklahoma is described by some as the "Buckle of the Bible Belt" and Washington state was more like a Babel of carnality by comparison.

The difference between these two ministries, from Bob's perspective, is very significant. When we study the two, it is like comparing Jacob with Israel, or Ishmael with Isaac. In the first instance, Bob felt that he was operating "in the flesh," now he feels that he is "in the Spirit."

The little church in Kirkland, Washington, has grown from 70 to 80 to over 3,000 in attendance. They achieved a measure of national prominence when they received a single day's offering in excess of 1.5 million dollars. At the time of this writing, they are still growing and now are in a building program costing in excess of $7,000,000.

The church there sponsors an annual meeting called "Peniel." They are quick to acknowledge that the power and growth which they have experienced comes not from men, but from God, and they are anxious to encourage others to experience this power too.

SPEWED OUT OF THE MOUTH

Juan Carlos Ortiz offers an interesting insight into Revelation 3:16, "So then because thou art lukewarm, and neither cold nor hot, I will spew thee out of my mouth . . ."

With his uncanny ability to use simple illustrations to bring light on profound truths, he describes the joy of taking a bite of charcoal broiled steak. It is delicious beyond description, but as it goes down his throat a dispute begins to take place. The gastric juices of his system want to take that bite of steak and destroy its identity. They want to completely break down and assimilate that bite of steak into his body. The bite of steak, however, has no intention of losing its own identity. The struggle between the two has a tendency to make the body very uncomfortable. As the choking sensation becomes more violent, the undigested food will go one way or the other. It will be assimilated into the body . . . or it will be spewed out.

The believer who insists on maintaining his or her own identity, his or her own plans, his or her own future, will be spewed out.

Being "filled with the Spirit" involves self crucifixion to the extent that Christ becomes all.

Paul expressed it beautifully,

> I am crucified with Christ: nevertheless I live; yet not I, but Christ liveth in me: and the life which I now live in the flesh I live by the faith of the Son of God, who loved me, and gave himself for me . . ." (Gal. 2:20).

THIS IS YOUR ROOM

On numerous occasions I have been a guest in someone elses house. Usually, I am shown the place which will be "my room" for the duration of my stay. Courtesy demands that I respect the privacy of my hosts. Because I have been invited as a guest in their home does not give me the right to wander into their private bedroom and start going through their dresser drawers.

I am a guest, but not a master. I do what I am told and respect the boundaries and limits which my hosts may place upon me.

Quite frequently, this is the way that we invite Jesus into our lives. We want Him as a guest, but we do not intend for Him to go wandering around in our personal areas or disrupting our personal plans.

Sometimes our experience of being "filled with the Spirit" is gradual and progressive.

We begin by inviting Jesus into the living room. After we become comfortable with Him there, we may let Him spend some time in the family room, or perhaps in the children's bedrooms. Some time later we may let Him into the kitchen, or the study where we keep our financial records, and perhaps ultimately into our own personal bedroom so that He becomes a part of the most intimate relationships of our lives.

Each time we invite Jesus into a new area of our lives, the only regret that we have is that we did not do it sooner. God is good! Those who trust their lives with Him will not only discover life, but life abundant! He needs to be invited into every area of our lives . . . not just as a guest . . . but as Lord of all!

. . . BE FILLED WITH THE SPIRIT . . .

In this book we have said much about subjectivism. We have tried to create an atmosphere of sensitivity and submission to the Spirit of God in every reader.

This section, however, should not be all that subjective. I do not know of any way that a sincere believer can read around or explain away this Biblical command,

> . . . and be not drunk with wine wherein is excess; but be filled with the Spirit . . .

Permit me to offer several suggestions which may help you to obey this Biblical command.

First of all, we need to be empty if we expect to be filled. You can't fill a bucket up with water if it is already full of something else. It seems that God's filling comes to fill the vacuum created when everything else, and everyone else has failed.

Secondly, we are told that God gives His Spirit to those who ask Him (Luke 11:13). The context of this Scripture involves the friend at midnight who received what he wanted because of his importunity and persistence. This is obviously the way we become filled with the Holy Spirit.

Thirdly, the Scriptures teach that God gives His Spirit to those that obey Him (Acts 5:32). It is remarkable how many people want the Holy Spirit, but have no desire to obey God. The "gift of the Holy Spirit" is associated, in particular, with the command to receive water baptism (Acts 2:38).

Fourthly, conversion is instantaneous, but transformation is a process. The one occurs immediately . . . the other takes place over the course of an entire lifetime. Our experiences with God grow more wonderful as our heart enlarges and grows. Being filled with the Spirit is not a one time experience which is never repeated . . . it is a progressive relationship which deepens and grows as we mature in Christ.

Finally, those who desire to be filled with the Spirit should get immediately involved in a deep and serious study of the Word of God. No contact which we have with the Spirit world is more reliable or better authenticated than the Holy Bible. There is no better way to comprehend the will of God or the mind of the Spirit than by the study of the Bible.

ONE SPIRIT

The Scriptures teach that, ". . . he that is joined unto the Lord is one spirit . . ." (I Cor. 6:17).

Just as husbands and wives become one on their wedding night, the believer becomes one with Jesus spiritually in the process of conversion. But husbands and wives go through many years of adjustment and development. The couple who celebrates their Golden Wedding Anniversary will probably be able to communicate on a deeper level and with greater understanding than they did many years before. Much of this communication is "nonverbal." So also the Holy Spirit is able to communicate nonverbally with those who are Christians.

One word which the Scriptures use to describe our relationships with Jesus is "fruit." Fruit is not just something which is seen externally, it is rather the outward manifestation of the inward nature. You do not gather grapes of thorns or figs of thistles.

Thus, when the Lord inhabits the temple of our earthly bodies, he transforms us from the works of the flesh to the fruit of the Spirit. We are not "conformed" by pressure from without. We are "transformed" by Jesus from within.

Sometimes it is difficult and perhaps even impossible for the Christian to determine which ideas came from his own mind . . . and which ideas came from the mind of the indwelling Spirit.

For he that is joined unto the Lord is one Spirit . . . let us be filled with Him!

THOUGHT QUESTIONS FOR CHAPTER VII

1. When seven men were selected to serve tables they were to be "full of the Holy Spirit . . ." (Acts 6:3). How did they tell which men were "full of the Holy Spirit"?
2. How can "spiritual" people be identified according to Galatians 6:1?
3. How often should one pray for the Holy Spirit (Luke 11:13)?
4. Compare people who are "drunk with wine to excess" and those who are "filled with the Spirit" (Eph. 5:18).
5. Compare "works" and "fruit" (Gal. 5:19ff.).
6. Why do some people argue so much about the Holy Spirit?
7. Discuss "nonverbal" communication and consider how the Holy Spirit may communicate with us "nonverbally."
8. Which is more important, Bible study or prayer?
9. Will a person "filled with the Holy Spirit" ever contradict the written Word of God in the Bible?
10. How can Bible study help us to be filled with the Spirit?

VIII

FORM AND POWER

. . . Having a form of godliness, but denying the power thereof . . . (II Tim. 3:5).

Down through the years, Christendom has accumulated a great many ideas and thought patterns which are not founded in the Word of God. Some of these traditions are harmless . . . and perhaps even beautiful. Others are so wrong that they make void the Word of God.

Here are a few examples of traditions which seem harmless to me . . . but which have no foundation in the Bible.

- Tradition teaches that there were three wise men . . . but the Bible does not say so. The Bible teaches that the wise men brought three gifts, but does not tell us how many wise men there were.

- Tradition teaches that the wise men brought their gifts to the Baby Jesus when He was in a manger . . . but the Bible does not say so. At the time the wise men came with their gifts, the Baby Jesus was in a house (Matt. 2:11).

- Tradition teaches that the angels "sang" on the night of Jesus' birth. The Bible does not say so. The Bible teaches that the angels were praising God and "saying" Glory to God in the Highest . . . (Luke 2:13-14).

- Etcetera.

These examples seem harmless to me. Our understanding . . . or misunderstanding of these stories does not alter any doctrine of salvation, divide any church, or form the basis of any denominational creed.

It is still our obligation to be like the noble Bereans and "search the Scriptures daily to see if these things are so" (Acts 17:11). Ignorance is not better than truth, and darkness is not better than light.

A PATTERN THEOLOGY

For many years I accepted the idea that there was a "divine pattern" for the New Testament Church. I believed and taught that the "true church" could be distinguished by an external form of church government.

The Scripture which I usually quoted to prove this position was Hebrews 8:5, ". . . make all things according to the pattern showed to thee in the mount . . ." This was what I had always heard. This was what I believed. But quite frankly, I had never studied the matter for myself. I had never examined and scrutinized this passage as I should have.

Under careful scrutiny this position seemed to vanish like a vapor. That Scripture teaches that Moses was given a divine pattern for the Tabernacle, but it does not teach that we are therefore given a divine pattern for the church. It is a quantum leap from the one position to the other.

In a previous work, *These Two Commandments,* I deal with the subject in greater detail than is necessary to repeat at this time (see pp. 94-98). After studying every example of every Greek word translated as "pattern" in the New Testament Scriptures, I have concluded that not one time do they refer to the governmental structure of our Lord's church.

Paul warned that in the last days men would be interested in a "form" of godliness . . . but would deny the "power" thereof. He seemed to be talking to me. I taught a great deal about "form" but said virtually nothing about "power."

POWER IN THE NEW TESTAMENT CHURCH

With a very minimum of investigation I soon discovered that the Bible had a lot more to say about power than I did. Here are a few examples:

- Jesus told His Apostles to wait for power - Acts 1:4-8.

- Peter insisted that miracles were performed by God's power - Acts 3:12.

- The Apostles gave witness of the resurrection with great power - Acts 4:33.

- Stephen was a man full of faith and power - Acts 6:8.

- Jesus was anointed with the Holy Spirit and power - Acts 10:38.

- Jesus was declared to be the Son of God with power - Rom. 1:4.

- The Gospel is the power of God unto salvation - Rom. 1:16.

- Paul's speech was not with enticing words of men's wisdom, but in the demonstration of the Spirit and of power - I Cor. 2:4.

- Paul wanted men's faith to be in the power of God - I Cor. 2:5.

91

- He wanted the Ephesians to have their eyes opened to the exceeding greatness of His power to us-ward who believe - Eph. 1:19.

- The power available to believers is able to accomplish above all that we can ask or think - Eph. 3:20.

- Paul sought to appropriate in his own life the power of the resurrection - Phil. 3:10.

- Paul prayed that the Colossians might be strengthened with all might according to His glorious power - Col. 1:11.

- The Gospel came to the Thessalonians not in word only, but in power - I Thess. 1:5.

- God's work in their midst was a work of faith with power - II Thess. 1:11.

- Paul wrote to Timothy that God had not given us a spirit of fear, but of power - II Tim. 1:7.

This is just a sampling of what the Bible says about power. It says a lot more about power than it ever does about form, and if we are to be a people of the Book we need to learn to speak where the Scriptures speak and also to speak as the Scriptures speak.

A PATTERN WITHOUT POWER

Several years ago I was invited to speak at a gathering of several hundred preachers, teachers, and Christian workers. Most of us had been infected with the idea that there was a divine pattern of external forms for the church consisting of elders, deacons, etc. and that any church not conforming to this "pattern" was a counterfeit church.

To illustrate what I think is the fallacy of this position, I approached them with a bit of duplicitly. I began talking to them about the "people of God in the First Century." Our theological mind-set led them to believe that I was talking about the "New Testament Church" and the "divine pattern" as had been done so many times before.

Instead of describing the New Testament Church, however, I began to describe a First Century synagogue. I did so in a way, however, that no one recognized the difference.

I said: The people of God in the First Century were . . .

- Separate from all idolatry and unbelievers
- Extremely evangelistic
- Baptized their converts only by immersion
- Met every week to study the Scriptures
- Their assemblies were presided over by elders who met high qualifications.
- Their assemblies also had deacons who met high qualifications.
- They supported the work of God with tithes and offerings.
- They did not allow a woman to teach or to usurp authority over a man.
- They gave a great emphasis to prayer.

etc.

The punch line came like this: And when you confessed Jesus in that group they kicked you out! This is stated explicitly in John 12:42. Many of the chief rulers believed on Jesus, but they wouldn't confess Him, lest they should be put out of the synagogue.

At the risk of making you weary with technical details, permit me to expound in greater detail about the Jewish synagogue.

The word "synagogue" is linguistically similar to the Bible word for church. "Sun" means "together" and "ago" means "to bring." Synagogue means "to bring together" and refers to an assembly of people. The Bible word for church is "ekklesia."

93

It comes from "ek" meaning "out of" and "kaleo" which means "to call." Both words are translated as "assembly" in the Scriptures.

The Jewish people were separate from all idolatry. As a people they never again bowed down to graven images following the Babylonian captivity.

The Jewish people were very evangelistic about their faith. Jesus said that they compassed sea and land to make a proselyte (Matt. 23:15). There were Jewish synagogues throughout virtually all of the Mediterranean World. The fact that Jesus said their converts became twofold more the child of hell than they were, still does not detract from their evangelistic fervor. They were indeed very evangelistic.

The Jewish people did practice a proselyte baptism, and this baptism was only by immersion.

The Jewish people did meet every week to study the Scriptures. They met, however, on the sabbath, or the seventh day of the week, while Christians assembled on the first day of the week (Acts 20:7).

The Jewish people did have elders and deacons in their synagogues, and the qualifications of these men are remarkably similar to those qualifications for elders and deacons in the New Testament Church.

The Jewish people did pay their tithes and offerings and even sounded trumpets to announce their generosity.

Women were not allowed to teach in the synagogues nor to usurp authority over a man.

The Jewish community did place a great emphasis on prayer, and some even stood out on the street corners and prayed to be seen of men.

An outward comparison between the church and the synagogue reveals that there were many external similarities. The early Christians did virtually all of these things which were commonplace in the synagogue.

Yet, Jesus taught that to attempt to mix these two into one would be like putting new wine in old skins, or new cloth in an old garment (Matt. 9:14-17). The two systems of religion were not compatible.

The difference was not so much something external, but something internal. The Christians possessed a power which was not available to the unconverted Jews in the synagogue.

POWER AND LOVE

On the night of His betrayal, Jesus instructed His disciples,

A new commandment I give unto you, That ye love one another; as I have loved you, that ye also love one another. By this shall all men know that ye are my disciples, if ye have love one to another (John 13:34-35).

It is significant to remember that at the time Jesus taught His disciples this lesson, they were arguing about which of them would be the greatest. He even had girded Himself about with a towel and washed their feet. After three years of teaching and training, however, they still lacked the power to love one another.

Jesus, therefore, taught them that it was expedient for them that He go away. As long as Jesus was in the flesh, He could only be one place at a time. If He was in Capernaum, He could not also be in Caesarea or Jerusalem.

When He became a Spirit, however, He would be able to be everywhere at the same time.

Jesus promised that He would not leave His disciples like orphans; he would go away to the Father and then He would return as a "comforter" or "helper." They would receive "power" after the Holy Spirit came upon them (Acts 1:8).

The word which Jesus used to describe the Holy Spirit is "paraklesis" and literally means someone whom you call along side to help. "Para" means "beside" and "kaleo" means "to call."

95

Jesus, by means of His Spirit, would come to His disciples and give them help and power to live the Christian life.

The primary work of the Spirit is not something external but something internal. We are not to be "conformed" but "transformed." The fruit of the Spirit is love, joy, peace, longsuffering, gentleness, goodness, faith, meekness, and temperance (Gal. 5:22-23). The Holy Spirit does not pressure us from without, but He transforms us from within.

When we "abide" in Jesus we draw from His power like a branch draws strength from the vine. Inasmuch as "fruit" is the outward expression of the inward nature, we manifest a new nature when we abide in Jesus.

It is not the outward form of our assemblies that convinces the world that we belong to Jesus . . . it is the transformation of our natures from within.

"By this shall all men know that ye are my disciples," said Jesus, "if ye have love one to another." This is the miracle of power which the world is waiting to see.

Virtually every nation on the face of the earth is torn by internal dissension. We are divided racially, socially, politically, economically, and religiously. But the power of the Spirit transforms us to be like Jesus. His power enables us to pray for those who despitefully use us and persecute us. We call upon God to forgive those who drive cruel nails into our hands and feet. We would rather suffer ourselves to be defrauded than to bring about disharmony and dissension in the precious Body of Jesus. We are known by our love!

EVANGELISM

When the focus is on "form" evangelism takes on an intellectual flavor. You have to roll up your intellectual sleeves and convince the skeptic that you have the right "form." It is something like a spiritual chess game. When the prospect is checkmated into the right position, he or she is considered to be the right kind of Christian.

I just had a lengthy discussion yesterday with a native of southeast Asia. He comes from a mountainous area where the tribal people are to a large extent illiterate and without formal education.

Our spiritual chess games mean little to such people. They would rather see a sermon than hear one any day. They would rather see the power of the Gospel transform an opium addict than to hear a theological debate on the meaning of some Greek word. They would rather see a singing convert set free from slavery to demon spirits than to hear a technical dissertation on church government.

The Mekane Yesus Lutheran Church of Ethiopia grew from 100,000 to over 500,000 in only two years time. A scholarly study by Lutheran researchers was done to understand the cause of such unprecedented church growth.

C. Peter Wagner tells about it in his excellent book, *On the Crest of the Wave.* The researchers stated:

> We thought they were responding because we were preaching the correct Lutheran doctrine of justification by faith. But now we know that it was not doctrine as such that was attracting their attention. It was the direct power of God in their everyday life that made the difference.

An overview of evangelism around the world will undoubtedly reveal the same truth. There are 12,000 people a day dying of starvation and malnutrition. The masses of the world are un-educated and illiterate. They are not interested in straining at spiritual gnats or splitting theological hairs. They are not attracted by the thousands to hear a doctor of theology wax eloquent on "why our church is the right church."

They are not interested in "forms of godliness" but in "power"!

CLEVERNESS OF SPEECH

A preacher who denies the power of God today will quite frequently resort to cleverness of speech in an attempt to get a crowd. "Catchy" sermon titles are mixed with promotional stunts that sometimes become bizarre and ridiculous.

Paul sought to distinguish his ministry from that of others who would "corrupt" the word of God (II Cor. 2:17). The Greek word translated as "corrupt" is "kapeleuo" which refers to a petty retailer or huckster. It is both unnecessary and inappropriate for a true preacher of the Gospel to hawk his wares like a huckster. The carnivals may come and go, but the gates of Hell shall not prevail against the church.

Summon all of your mental and spiritual energies into one place and consider again Paul's words to the Corinthians.

> And I, brethren, when I came to you, came not with excellency of speech or of wisdom, declaring unto you the testimony of God. For I determined not to know any thing among you, save Jesus Christ, and him crucified. And I was with you in weakness, and in fear, and in much trembling. And my speech and my preaching was not with enticing words of man's wisdom, but in demonstration of the Spirit and of power: That your faith should not stand in the wisdom of men, but in the power of God (I Cor. 2:1-5).

A classic example of a con man comes from a previous generation and is found in the person of the late "Death Valley Scotty."

Scotty was a master of promotion and manipulation. In April of 1902, he walked boldly into a banker's office with two gold nuggets. He claimed that the gold had come from a mine in Death Valley. He gave the location of the mine as "130 miles southwest of Fenner." This actually missed Death Valley by some 100 miles. During the next four years, however, that banker invested some $10,000 in the "Death Valley Mine," but never had anything more to show for his money than two gold nuggets and a pile of correspondence.

When Scotty would get his hands on a grub stake, he would "invest" it in the most unusual ways. For example, in 1905 he deposited $4,000 with the Sante Fe Railroad to hire a special train from California to Chicago. The only two passengers on the train were Scotty and a mongrel dog. He claimed to have paid $1,000 for the dog's collar, and wanted to take him for a ride. Naturally, the newspapers were properly informed . . . crowds lined the tracks . . . headlines screamed the story . . . and Scotty became a national sensation.

One wealthy investor built a castle in Death Valley and let Scotty claim that it was his. When they installed the organ in the castle the rumor was out that they played the organ to keep people from hearing the sounds of workers mining for gold beneath the castle itself.

Scotty's fame became his undoing. His estranged wife read about him in the papers. She had not received support from him in years and took him to court assuming that he was rich. She was wrong! It was all a scam. He was a fraud. There was a lot of smoke, but no fire.

All Scotty had to offer was "cleverness of speech" . . . there was no substance to his remarks. He was a master at promotion . . . but he had no power. He could get a crowd . . . but he had to use the methods of a huckster to do so.

We are today in the midst of a worldwide revival, and the substance of that revival is not "cleverness of speech" as our next chapter will point out.

God is not just a great God of yesterday . . . and a great God of tomorrow . . . He is a great God today!

THOUGHT QUESTIONS FOR CHAPTER VIII

1. How did Paul's preaching involve "power" instead of "cleverness of speech"?
2. Would Paul use the same approach if he were preaching in the 20th century?
3. Is it wrong for a church to use contests to grow? Should it be necessary?

4. Was Paul's comparison of Macedonia and Achaia in II Corinthians 9 like a contest?
5. Some say, "What you win them with is what you win them to." Discuss!
6. Will we be judged by God as individuals . . . or groups? (See Rev. 2:18-29.)
7. How did the First Century Church differ from the Jewish synagogue?
8. How does the Holy Spirit produce "fruit" in our lives?
9. How can we achieve "power" in our ministry?
10. How would this "power" help us to do God's work?

IX

SIGNS AND WONDERS

Through mighty signs and wonders by the power of the Spirit of God; so that from Jerusalem, and round about unto Illyricum, I have fully preached the gospel of Christ (Rom. 15:19).

In a brief ten years of time, the Apostle Paul had "fully preached" the gospel of Christ from Jerusalem and round about unto Illyricum. Therefore, "having no more place in these parts" (vs. 23) he desired to come by Rome on his journey to Spain.

The remarkable growth of the gospel was due in part to proper techniques, to much hard work, and also to political, social, and religious circumstances which helped set the stage for evangelism. It cannot be denied, however, that "mighty signs and wonders" didn't hurt anything. As a matter of fact, as Paul reflected on the growth of the Gospel, he associated it with "mighty signs and wonders by the power of the Spirit of God."

A study of church growth in the twentieth century might also reveal the same.

The July 11, 1986 issue of *Christianity Today* contains a fascinating article entitled, "Where in the World is the Church Growing?" A color coded map reflecting growth rates around the world places mainland China, Brazil, Guatemala, Costa Rica and other "third world" countries in the highest category.

When Christian missionaries were expelled from China in 1949-50, there were only approximately 1,000,000 Chinese believers. Today it has been conservatively estimated that there are between 30-50 million believers in mainland China and some feel that there may be as many as 100 million. This has happened in spite of the fact that the greatest bloodbath in human history occurred in China during the same period of time, and Christians, in particular, were victims of the holocaust. It seems that the amazing growth of Christianity in China cannot be explained without an element of the supernatural.

Christianity Today tells about a miraculous healing in Zhejiang Province and then adds:

> The experience of the Zhejiang villagers is not unusual. Healings, exorcisms, and other supernatural signs and wonders have accompanied phenomenal growth of the church not only in China, but in many other parts of the world. In fact, the church around the world is growing in ways that have seldom before been seen.

Leslie Lyall, in his book *God Reigns in China,* estimates that in the three years following 1980 as many as 27,000 people per day may have become Christians in China.

Donald McGavran was a Christian Church missionary before founding the Fuller School of World Mission. He is quoted in Peter Wagner's book, *On the Crest of the Wave,* as saying:

> I do not come from a church background that emphasizes healing. In fact we have been a bit critical of it. . . . The evidence I uncovered in country after country—and in North America

as well—simply wouldn't permit me to hold my former point of view. And I may say that as I meditated on it, my biblical conviction also wouldn't permit it (p. 131).

Those of us who believe that the Bible is inspired of God sometimes grow weary with people who reject it's message purely on the basis of preconceptions and prejudice. We correctly argue that before one rejects the miracles of the Bible he ought to be honest enough to at least consider the evidence. Perhaps the time has come for us to practice what we preach. Why should we reject the accounts of modern miracles without first considering the evidence?

We, who are Children of the light, should not be afraid of the light. We are commanded in Scripture to "prove all things" (I Thess. 5:21). The Greek word translated as "prove" is one which is used with reference to the assaying of metals. We are to "prove all things" and then: "hold fast that which is good, (and abstain from all appearances of evil. . . .''

In 1974 Peter Wagner taught a workshop at the Lausanne congress stressing the urgency of planting new churches. Afterward a Nigerian came up and thanked him. He said that the Lord had enabled him to start 258 new churches in the previous five years with an estimated 34,000 believers. Such a dramatic harvest of souls is apparently not something unusual in our generation. We seem to be in the midst of a world wide revival, and unfortunately, some of us like Rip VanWinkle, are sleeping through the revolution.

In 1983, Regal Books published *On the Crest of the Wave,* by Peter Wagner. At that time he indicated that there were 78,000 more believers every day (p. 19). This was not a figure drawn wishfully out of the air, but a studied conclusion based upon statistical evidence.

He points out that 100 years ago there were no churches in Korea. Now there are 6,000 in the city of Seoul alone and six new churches are started in South Korea every day. These churches include the largest Methodist church in the world, the

103

largest Presbyterian Church in the world, and also the largest church of any church in the world.

Wagner was himself a missionary to Bolivia for sixteen years. During all of that time on the mission field he did not see any signs of miracles. The evidence he encounters today, however, is causing him to have second thoughts. He writes:

> Why is it that we American evangelicals have not really believed in the immediate power of the Holy Spirit in miracles and wonders? Oh, most of us believed it intellectually because we read about it in the Bible. But it did not play much of a part, if any, in our daily lives or in our churches. I now think that a good deal of the problem is the pervasive influence of secular humanism in our American culture" (p. 129).

It may very well be that Wagner is right. Many of us have arrived at preconceived notions on the basis of a theological bias. We have our minds made up and sometimes resent anyone trying to confuse us with the facts.

THE MORSE FAMILY

It has been my good fortune to be personally acquainted with the family of J. Russell Morse. They have been missionaries laboring in Asia since 1921 and are among the most famous Christian workers in the world. The *Reader's Digest* and other national and international publications have featured articles about their outstanding work.

A book by Eugene Morse, *Exodus to a Hidden Valley,* was published by *Reader's Digest* and condensed in their February 1974 issue.

In more than sixty years on the mission field this family has seen dozens, and perhaps even hundreds of miraculous answers to prayer. Permit me to share just one. The fact that this story was recorded in the *Reader's Digest* will give it a certain measure of credibility with some people. We know that this popular publication is not inspired, but its editors do have an outstanding track record. They researched the book about the Morses for a year before going into print.

The essence of the miracle was this. Several thousand refugees were trapped in Hidden Valley, high up in the Himalayan Mountains. On the verge of starvation they found their rice crop threatened by a plague of caterpillars.

They had no sprays or insecticides . . . literally nowhere to turn but to God. They had picked bushels of caterpillars by hand, they had released their chickens in the fields . . . they had tried everything within their power . . . and had failed.

Finally they assembled their preachers, teachers, elders, deacons, and song leaders to decide on a course of action. Like Elijah confronting the priests of Baal they determined to challenge the caterpillars by the power of God.

Together with at least one person from each affected family they went from field to field praising God and crying out for deliverance.

Within three days the plague was gone. They heard on their radio that the same or similar plague had destroyed thousands of acres in lower Burma, and no insecticides seemed to be effective against it.

Now the conscientious reader is faced with a decision. Do we summarily disregard this story as a fabrication, do we consider it a coincidence, or do we accept it as a miracle from God? Pharaoh saw a whole series of miracles without surrendering his heart to God. Let us give diligence to guard against hardening our hearts like the Pharaoh.

Not everyone is sensitive to spiritual things. Zacharias, the father of John the Baptist, for example, spoke with an angel and yet did not believe. His wife, by contrast, simply felt her baby move within her womb and was filled with the Holy Spirit. We need to be sensitive to even little and insignificant inward feelings as she was.

One tremendous asset in discerning the power of God is the ability to reason. Sometimes we get in such a hurry that we fail to stop and reflect upon unusual circumstances. Balaam, for example, got so mad at his donkey that he was ready to kill it. At that point God opened the animal's mouth and he began to reason with the wayward prophet:

> Am I not thine ass, upon which thou hast ridden ever since I was thine unto this day? Was I ever wont to do so unto thee? (Num. 22:30).

When Balaam stopped to think about the unusual things happening right before him, God opened his eyes and he saw an angel standing in the way with a drawn sword.

What do you suppose God will have to do to us before we will slow down long enough to really consider some of the unusual things happening around us?

DR. GARLAND BARE

Dr. Garland Bare is quoted several times in this book. His name is synonymous with integrity to all who know him. He has lived a life of faith and can tell stories by the hour about answers to prayer.

Among the most remarkable experiences of his life was a miraculous healing which took place in Pua, Thailand in 1973.

A young man named Ban Chong wanted to become a Christian. His father was a witch-doctor and forbade him to do so. In order to keep him away from the influence of the missionaries Ban Chong was banished to the mountains for a year to care for the cattle. Here he was stricken with falciparum malaria and was brought to the hospital where Dr. Bare was practicing.

For some forty eight hours Dr. Bare used every new medical treatment and technique available, but to no avail. Ban Chong only became worse.

Finally, as a last resort, they began dripping quinine into his veins. At this point the patient began to hemorrhage in his digestive tract and bladder. The condition was described as "black water fever" as it causes the urine to turn black.

106

Dr. Bare then gave Ban Chong a transfusion. In that remote area only one suitable donor could be found . . . and he weighed but 90 lbs. One unit of blood was given . . . but it did no good.

By now Ban Chong's blood pressure was 80/20. His family was summoned to his bedside and informed that he was dying. His witch-doctor father came with his brother, Jur Sha, who was a Christian elder.

Father - "Can God heal my son"?

Dr. Bare - "God can do all things!"

Father - "If he becomes a Christian will that guarantee his healing?"

Dr. Bare - "No!"

Father - "One year ago I forbade him to become a Christian, but now I am willing if he wants to."

Ban Chong - "It is too late . . . I am dying."

Dr. Bare - "You can give what is left of your life to God."

Ban Chong - "I can't pray . . . I have on the spirit strings." (Spirit strings are articles associated with demon worship. By now Ban Chong's blood pressure was 50/0 . . . his extremities were cold and his eyes were glazed. Dr. Bare asked for scissors and removed the spirit strings.)

Ban Chong - "God, I am dying. If it is at all possible save me!"

At this point Dr. Bare said that immediately Ban Chong's color returned to his face and his bloated stomach became flat. Dr. Bare asked for a blood pressure reading and the nurse said it was 120/70 . . . his pulse was 80 and regular . . . and he had no more fever or other symptoms of malaria.

Since it was late Friday night Ban Chong remained in the hospital until morning and then was released a well man. On Sunday he was baptized into Christ along with his father and other members of the family.

Dr. Bare states that one of the interesting ironies of the story is that the miracle was recorded at the hospital by an unbelieving nurse. Not only was she not a Christian, she had been openly antagonistic to the Gospel. After witnessing this event, however, she ceased her opposition to Christianity . . . but still did not give her heart to Christ.

I personally believe this story. I think all who know Dr. Garland Bare will believe it too. If you do not believe this story you ought to at least examine the motives for your unbelief. Is it a lack of evidence which causes you to doubt, or is it a humanistic view of God? Surely the rational mind must conclude that all things are possible with God!

BRAZIL

According to *Christianity Today,* Brazil is among the countries of the world where Christianity is growing at the greatest rate. It was my privilege to visit there several years ago and speak at a missionary conference.

When the conference was over Gerry Laxen and I took several days and visited missionaries throughout the country. Just before returning to the States we were privileged to spend a day in Sao Paulo.

My reason for visiting this beautiful city was to see first hand a little group of believers who prayed. David Sanders told me about them. At the time he was a veteran of thirty five years on the mission field. He had been called to Sao Paulo some time before to baptize 37 people into Christ. He was not certain just how all these people were converted to Christ, except that there was a woman who prayed. She had no theological training, but apparently had so many prayers answered that people were coming to Christ as a result.

When we arrived I was delighted to discover that a prayer meeting was scheduled in her home that very night. It was a large home in a very nice part of town. Since preacher counts are notoriously exaggerated I counted chairs before anyone arrived. There were 96 chairs.

When the meeting began I observed that every chair was occupied and some parents were holding small children on their laps. There were also people standing, and people listening from outside. There were easily over 100 people present.

K.O. Backstrand used to say, with a certain amount of sarcasm, that one way to call some churches to order is to ask for testimonies. In some places when you do that it will get so quiet that you can hear a pin drop. This was not the way it was in Sao Paulo.

After singing a group of spirited praise choruses the smiling and excited converts began sharing their testimonies. Bro. Sanders translated for me. One man said that he had leukemia . . . until he came to Sister Fonseca. He claimed he was healed. A woman stood up and told about her divorce. Her estranged husband had refused for years to give her any support . . . until she came to Sister Fonseca for prayer. Within three days the money began to arrive. The testimonies continued for more than an hour. I was invited to share a few words with them . . . they had a Bible lesson . . . and prayer. It was after 11:00 p.m. before the people began to leave.

Sister Fonseca had been mixed up in the occult for fifteen years . . . and so had many of her converts. They were discovering, however, that there was power in the name of Jesus which they had not known in their former life. At the time I was there the number of believers had already grown to 400 . . . and they didn't even have a preacher or a place in which to meet.

It reminded me of Paul's experience in Ephesus when thousands came to Christ out of the occult. The Scriptures put it like this:

> Many that believed came, and confessed, and shewed their deeds. Many of them also which used curious arts brought their books together, and burned them before all men: and they counted the price of them, and found it fifty thousand pieces of silver. So mightily grew the word of God and prevailed (Acts 19:18-20).

ANGELS AND DEMONS

We live in an age when thousands of American citizens are fascinated with the occult. Books on the subject are frequently among the best sellers and libraries have long waiting lists of people who want to check them out.

Preachers of the Gospel believe in a real Devil and have some grave reservations about the many people who place themselves in the sphere of his influence and power.

I have spoken with a considerable number of missionaries who claim to have seen the power of demons manifest on the mission field. Things happen that for all intents and purposes reflect the supernatural.

Isn't it strange, however, that we are sometimes more prone to believe in a supernatural Devil than we are in a supernatural God. We steer clear of books and paraphernalia about the occult, for we properly fear their power . . . yet we are sometimes reluctant to believe in the reality of angels or the miracle working power of prayer.

Let us state categorically: "Greater is he that is in you, than he that is in the world (I John 4:4).

If the Devil has the power to work the supernatural in our day and age, then God has more power.

Many parents are placing their children in Christian schools or are home schooling, because they fear the pervasive influence of humanism. It tints and shades our thinking in sometimes very subtle ways. Every church believes in prayer, but not all churches believe in answers to prayer. Perhaps the pervasive influence of humanism has affected us more than we are willing to admit.

In many places it is completely orthodox and expected to pray for the sick . . . if they ever start getting healed, however, you're apt to be in trouble.

NO MIGHTY WORK

Virtually everyone within the framework of Christendom believes in the miraculous power of Christ. We may not feel comfortable believing in miraculous power today, but certainly it was manifest 2,000 years ago when Jesus walked upon the earth.

It is interesting, however, to note that there were places where even Jesus could do no mighty works.

As incredible as it might seem, it was in His own hometown of Nazareth. These were the people more familiar with the flesh of Jesus than any other. When He stood up to speak they recognized Him as the carpenter who had lived and worked in their midst for almost 30 years. They knew that His mother's name was Mary, and that His brothers were James, and Joses, and Juda, and Simon. They knew that His sisters still lived in the area.

They were so familiar with the veil, that it prevented them from going "beyond the veil."

For this reason the Scriptures teach, "AND HE COULD THERE DO NO MIGHTY WORK." Oh, He did lay His hands upon a few sick folk and heal them, but the mighty manifestations of His power which were seen elsewhere, were impossible to perform in Nazareth. Their drenching doubt and pessimism smothered out the flames of His miracle working power.

Even Jesus could not do mighty works in Nazareth!

How is it in your town? How is it in your congregation?

The Scriptures beckon us to enter in boldly into the holiest of all by the blood of Jesus. We are to enter in through that new and living way which He hath consecrated for us, through the veil . . . that is to say . . . His flesh!

THOUGHT QUESTIONS FOR CHAPTER IX

1. Why do some deny that the miracles recorded in the Bible are true?
2. What can be done to get such people to consider the evidence for believing the Bible?
3. Why do some people deny the existence of miracles today?

4. What can be done to get such people to consider evidence today?
5. What part did "signs and wonders" have to do with Paul's efforts at evangelism?
6. In your judgment is there really a wave of evangelism around the world or is someone just making up all these stories?
7. Discuss the situation at Nazareth which made it impossible for Jesus to do mighty works there.
8. Why do you suppose there is such an interest today in the occult?
9. How can we demonstrate that Jesus is more powerful than the Devil?
10. If God worked a miracle in your life, who would object?

X

REAPING WHERE YOU BESTOWED NO LABOR

I sent you to reap that whereon ye bestowed no labor . . . (John 4:38).

As members of the human race we are prone to see things from a human point of view. From the human point of view, if it "sounds too good to be true . . . it probably is." From the human point of view, you "pay for what you get." From the human point of view, you "reap what you sow."

Jesus, however, tried to give His disciples something other than a human point of view. When we are "born again" we no longer see things as we did before. Those who are born from above are citizens of a heavenly kingdom with perceptions in the spirit world not available to those who are merely born of the flesh.

Jesus sent out His disciples to reap that whereon they had bestowed no labor. Someone else had done the work . . . they reaped the harvest.

As a training exercise He sent them forth with:

no gold

no silver

no brass

no wallet

no extra coat

no extra shoes

and no staff (Matt. 10:9-10).

When they returned they had found God to be faithful. All of the things which they so desperately needed had been graciously provided.

The Bible gives many examples of this spiritual principle.

When Philip stood by a deserted roadway between Jerusalem and Gaza, the Ethiopian eunuch came by. At the time he drew near to Philip, he was reading the fifty-third chapter of Isaiah. The man was ready to become a Christian, but Philip had virtually nothing to do with his preparation. He was ripe for harvest. In a short time he had been baptized into Christ and went on his way rejoicing (Acts 8:26-40).

When Peter arrived at the household of Cornelius the whole family was eagerly awaiting the opportunity to become Christians. Someone else had done the work and Peter was merely reaping the harvest (Acts 10).

When Ananias was commissioned to preach to Saul of Tarsus, he didn't want to do it. He said,

> Lord, I have heard by many of this man, how much evil he hath done to thy saints at Jerusalem: and here he hath authority from the chief priests to bind all that call on thy name (Acts 9:13-14).

Ananias had nothing to worry about. God had already prepared Saul's heart. Saul even had received a vision of a man named Ananias laying hands on him that he might receive his sight. He was reaping that upon which he had bestowed no labor.

Saul himself would also become a beneficiary of this principle. We know him best not as Saul of Tarsus, but as Paul the Apostle. As Paul started out to witness for His Lord, he found at every juncture precisely the personnel and resources which he needed to be successful.

God pointed out Timothy to him through prophetic utterances (I Tim. 1:18).

God directed him to Troaz where he met Luke the beloved physician (Acts 16:1ff.).

God gave him a vision of a man from Macedonia pleading for help (Acts 16:9).

God sent an earthquake to bring about the conversion of the Philippian jailer (Acts 16:19-40).

Paul himself would testify, "Not that we are sufficient of ourselves to think anything as of ourselves, but our sufficiency is of God" (II Cor. 3:5). Paul did not rely upon enticing words of man's wisdom, but in the demonstration of the Spirit and of power (I Cor. 2:4).

ETERNITY IN THEIR HEARTS

One of the most provocative books I have read in recent years is the excellent book, *Eternity in their Hearts,* by Don Richardson. Richardson became world famous when his book, *Peace Child,* was condensed in the *Reader's Digest.* He had also written *Lords of the Earth,* and is widely recognized for his anthropological and linguistic work among the Sawi people of Irian Jaya.

"Eternity in their hearts" is a phrase found in Ecclesiastes 3:11 which indicates that God has placed eternity in the hearts of men. Richardson relates more than twenty-five incredible, but true accounts of peoples all over the world who are eagerly waiting for someone to come and tell them of the One True God.

When Canadian Albert Brant and his colleague, Glen Cain, went to Ethiopa in 1948, their mission work was off to a running start. The reason . . . a man named Warrasa Wange, from the royal family of the Gedeo tribe, had received a vision. In his vision he saw two white men erect flimsy shelters under a large sycamore tree near his home in Dilla. Later they built shiny roofed structures. Eventually these structures covered the entire hillside. Wange had never seen anything up to this point but grass roofed huts. In the vision, Wange was instructed that these men would have a message from the One True God. When these white skinned missionaries put up their tent under a large sycamore tree near Dilla, they were in for a most pleasant surprise. They would reap that upon which they had bestowed no labor.

When William Marcus Young climbed out of a well that he was digging and spoke to representatives from the Wa tribe in Asia, he, too, was in for a pleasant surprise.

These Wa tribesmen were sent by their leader, Pu Chan, to search for a white man with a book from God. A pony had been saddled and released with the belief that it would lead them to the man they were seeking. They had followed the pony over 200 miles of mountainous trails to the city of Kentung. Here the pony had stopped by the very well which William Marcus Young was digging.

His granddaughter, Nelda Widlund, related to Richardson that the Wa messengers asked, "Have you brought a book of God?" When Young nodded they were so overcome with emotion that they fell at his feet and announced, "This pony is saddled especially for you. Our people are all waiting. Fetch the book! We must be on our way!" (p. 103).

Experiences like this are being repeated all over the world!

DR. GARLAND BARE - THAILAND

Since Dr. Bare is a personal acquaintance of the Young family, and since he labored many years for Christ in the same area, I take the liberty of quoting him again at this time.

116

Dr. Bare is at this time serving as a staff physician with the University of Nebraska in Lincoln, Nebraska and will be well known to many who read this book. Our knowledge of him, his work, and his integrity, will be a strong confirmation of this principle.

In 1955, Brother Bare pioneered in evangelizing the Khamu tribe in the Nan Province of Northern Thailand. It was an area where the Gospel had never been preached, and as far as we know, there were no converts to Christ among the Khamu people. These people were noted for the intensity of their demon worship and were a rather withdrawn and reserved tribe. One might imagine that it would take many years to bring such people to a saving knowledge of the Lord Jesus Christ. Brother Bare found otherwise.

On his initial visit, the headman of the village gave him permission to stay in his home. It was a typical dwelling for that part of the world, merely a thatched roofed hut elevated on stilts to protect you from wild animals.

After dark when the people of the village came in from the fields they gathered to hear the white man. Garland was wise indeed to "hear" before he spoke. He asked them about their beliefs and discovered that the primary focus of their worship involved evil spirits. These evil spirits were blamed for every illness, every natural disaster, every crop failure, and worship among the Khamu people consisted of attempting to appease these evil spirits.

"Are there any good spirits?" Brother Bare asked. "Yes!" they replied. There was a Good Spirit which their ancestors had told them about, but they had lost contact with Him.

He asked them if they knew where the world came from. They said that they did. They believed that there was a Great Creator God, but their ancestors had lost all the books about Him in a great flood . . . and they knew that this Creator Spirit was good.

117

Garland said, "I have good news for you. The Great Creator God has sent His Son to the earth to make contact with His people."

They responded with such excitement that they asked him to stay on in their village and tell them more. Within a month three families turned to the Lord . . . five more families soon followed. These were the first converts to Jesus ever among the Khamu people in Nan Province . . . and the harvest came from seeds planted in ages past.

GIL CONTRERAS - MEXICO

When Gil Contreras started for Mexico City as a missionary almost 30 years ago, he knew only one person in that vast city . . . and she moved before he and his family arrived.

The success of the work is so much the result of God's work that Brother Contreras illustrates his ministry by telling the story of a flea riding upon the horn of a huge ox. When someone asked the flea what he was doing he replied, "We're plowing."

The work in Oaxaca opened up because a man from that area wrote repeatedly pleading for someone to come to them and preach.

The work in Veracruz was off and running when someone contacted Brother Contreras to inform him that some 50 people were waiting on him to come and baptize them.

It was my own good pleasure to visit the work among the Otomi Indians in the mountains above Mexico City. This was an area so violent that when a police officer arrived to restore the peace they shot him, tied him on his horse, and sent him back to town.

When the militia arrived the Indians merely vanished into the mountains and waited for them to leave.

Through the interpreter these people described to me the horrors of their life before the Gospel came.

Brother Contreras, however, was not the real pioneer in this particular work. He actually reaped what someone else had sown. God arranged it so that literally hundreds of converts and several congregations were given over to him that he might teach them.

Gil and the Lord are "still plowing"!

ZIDEN NUTT - AFRICA

The year was 1961. Twenty-five year old Ziden Nutt had only been two short months in Africa as a missionary when he took an interpreter and drove four hours into the bush for an historic meeting with an African Chieftan named Dendawa.

Chief Dendawa was the Paramount Chief over some 250,000 subjects and five wives. Six lesser chiefs served under his jurisdiction. He had earned the reputation of being inhospitable to Christianity for he had consistently turned down every church and every missionary that had asked his permission to enter the area.

One is never permitted to approach such a chief without following the proper protocol. Ziden had sent an appropriate gift in an appropriate way and waited for the chief to reciprocate. After some time Ziden's gift was accepted and he was granted an audience.

It was not a private audience, but all of the important men from the area were present. It was an august assembly of 600 or 700 men . . . all of them armed with axes and spears or other weapons.

Ziden felt a tenseness which seemed to run deeper than the normal barriers of language and culture. Later he would discover that virtually all of these men were opposed to letting a white man come into their area. They had never forgotten those stories of the slave traders who carried away their wives and children in a previous generation.

The chief, speaking through an interpreter, asked Ziden just two questions.

First of all he said, "Who is the head of your church?"

119

Secondly, "Who makes the laws for your church?"

The chief apparently possessed a discernment about denomi-nationalism which was quite profound.

Ziden answered both questions in a straightforward and simple manner which he felt the chief would understand.

First of all, he explained that only God was the head of the church. The chief knew God at that time only as "Denga Denga" or the Spirit from Above. There was no earthly head or potentate to the church of the living God.

Secondly, he displayed to the chief a small Bible and explained that this book came from the Great Spirit and was the only rule of faith and practice which he would follow.

The chief immediately leaped to his feet and began shouting, "Where have you been . . . why didn't you come before?"

Further inquiry revealed that this chief had been waiting since 1937 for someone to come into his area who would answer those two questions in the way that Ziden did.

Today, this area which is now called "Chidamoyo" has some 105 indigenous congregations, five schools and a hospital.

Ziden is quick to give God the glory. He was reaping benefits which he did not sow.

We now know that at least a part of the groundwork and preparation for the work in Chidamoyo was done by courageous missionaries from Australia and New Zealand. In particular, Ziden feels a debt of gratitude to a missionary named Ray Knapp. It was he who taught Chief Dendawa's nephew the beauty of Jesus and the blessings of non-denominational Christianity. When Brother Knapp died the Africans honored his memory by inscribing the word "RUDO" upon his grave. This is their word for love.

Jesus Christ is the Head of His Body, the church. The mem-bers of that blessed Body circle the globe and span the centuries of time so that we are never isolated from those who have gone before, or those who will follow after.

Some of us plant . . . some of us water . . . but it is God who gives the increase!

GERALD HOLMQUIST - BRAZIL

Gerald Holmquist is a veteran of more than 20 years on the mission field in Brazil. He told me recently of an experience in which he was able to reap where others had sown.

Gerald and his wife were working in Anapolis, but feeling that perhaps the time had come for them to move into another area. At this point, Gerald took a brief tour checking up on previous converts who had moved out of the area.

In the course of his journey he visited Samuel Carneiro de Castro who had moved to Itapuranga and was director of the local branch of the Bank of Brazil. Samuel begged him to come and start a work in Itapuranga. After considerable prayer, Gerald and his wife, Mary, answered that call. That was in April of 1985.

By the time that the Holmquists arrived on the field, Samuel had built and paid for a building that would seat 300 . . . He had printed invitations to 500 leaders in the community . . . and when Gerald arrived for their first church service on November 23, 1985, there were over 500 in attendance.

Someone else did the plowing, planting and cultivation . . . Gerald came to do the reaping . . . and God gave the increase.

CAN GOD GIVE YOU GUIDANCE?

Yes! There is absolutely no question but what God can give you guidance. It may not do you any good, however, unless you are on the move. The controls on an airplane may work perfectly, but they do not affect the plane unless the plane is moving. A rocket doesn't need guidance until it blasts off.

Yes! God can give you guidance. Undoubtedly, He has given you guidance many, many times in the past. Sometimes we are not even aware of this guidance. We dig our toe in the dirt and cry "tough luck" without understanding that our wonderful God was trying to get our attention. We wipe our tears and ask "why?" when we ought to be smiling and saying "why not?"

121

The greatest journey begins with a single step. Why not determine today to begin some venture in faith. Abram began his journey "not knowing where he was going." It was in the process of that journey that God guided him to the promised land.

Why not get on the move? We have a divine invitation to enter into the Holiest by the blood of Jesus. Take that first important step . . . TODAY!

THOUGHT QUESTIONS FOR CHAPTER X

1. Why do you suppose Jesus sent out His Disciples without any provisions?
2. Why didn't God tell Abram where he was going before he left (Heb. 11:8)?
3. What good is guidance to something which is not moving?
4. What happens to that which is "ripe" but is not harvested? Is this also true of souls?
5. How do we as human beings communicate "nonverbally"?
6. How could God communicate with us "nonverbally"?
7. How can an experienced tracker follow a trail which others cannot see?
8. How can an experienced mechanic hear engine noises which others cannot discern?
9. How do we exercise our senses to discern good and evil (Heb. 5:14)?
10. If God wanted to lead us today to witness to someone who is ready to become a Christian, how would He do it?

XI

DANGEROUS PRAYERS

Pray ye therefore the Lord of the harvest, that he will send forth laborers into his harvest (Matt. 9:38).

This certainly seemed like an innocent and harmless request. Anyone can pray!

The problem with praying, however, is that sometimes God calls upon us to answer our own prayers . . . or sometimes He brings upon us such pain and distress that we are almost literally thrust out of our lethargy into the work of His harvest.

In the Scripture before us it is important to remember that Jesus sent out the very disciples into the harvest whom He had asked to pray about the harvest.

A closer examination of the Scripture provides an interesting insight into the way that God sometimes chooses to work.

W. E. Vine in his "Expository Dictionary of New Testament Words" lists 12 different Greek words which are all translated as "send" in the New Testament Scriptures. Each of these words has its own particular emphasis so that the meaning of our Lord might be understood with a certain measure of precision.

The word before us is "ekballo." It is a compound of two different Greek words. "Ballo" means to "throw" and "ek" means "out." It literally means to "throw out."

Fifty-two times it is translated as "cast out" in the King James Version of the Bible.

Thayer in his Greek English Lexicon defines the word, "with the included notion of more or less violence."

This is the word used to describe the cleansing of the temple when Jesus "cast out" the moneychangers (Matt. 21:12; Mark 11:15; John 2:15).

This is the word used to describe the way that Paul and Barnabas were driven out of Antioch in Pisidia (Acts 13:40).

This is the word used to describe the way that Sarah wanted Abraham to "cast out" Hagar and her son (Gal. 4:30).

This is the word used to describe Diotrephes who prated against the Apostles with malicious words. He would not receive the brethren, and "cast out" those who did (III John 10).

This is the word used to describe the way that Jesus was "driven" into the wilderness to be tempted of the Devil (Mark 1:12).

There may be instances when the word reflects less violent actions than others, but it is indeed a special word which seems to have some very strong connotations. The word is used in James 2:25 to describe the way that Rahab sent out the spies another way. Rahab did not literally "drive out" or "cast out" those spies. Yet, the circumstances surrounding that incident were very powerful indeed.

As you will recall, the king of Jericho was searching for the spies of Joshua and undoubtedly would have tortured them to obtain information, and in all probability would have then had them put to death if he could have only found them.

Rahab, in the meantime, had hidden them under stalks of flax upon her roof. Having instructed the soldiers to search in the wrong direction, she "sent out" the spies another way. No one can read the story without feeling some of the urgency and emotion which must have been experienced at the time.

There is a certain danger associated with praying that the Lord "send" for laborers into his harvest. He may send us! He may create such discomfort for us in our present circumstances that we would be almost literally "cast out" into the work which He has for us to do.

An unknown author has captured the meaning of this Scripture in this beautiful piece of poetry.

IT'S DANGEROUS TO PRAY

I prayed, Oh Lord, bless all the world,
    And help me do my part.
And straightway he commanded me,
    "Bind up a broken heart."
I prayed, Oh bless each hungry child,
    May they be amply fed.
Then God said, "Go find a starving soul and
    Share with him your bread."
Oh, stir the hearts of men, I prayed
    And make them good and true.
God answered quickly, "There is one way,
    I stir men's hearts through you."
Dear friend, unless you really mean
    Exactly what you say,
Until you mean to work for God,
    It's dangerous to pray.

RANDY CARLSON

The first time I remember seeing Randy Carlson, he was walking across the campus of a Christian college. The person next to me said, "There's that kid who is dying of cancer."

Randy was indeed a cancer patient. He had gone through the sad cycle of surgery, radiation, and chemotherapy, but nothing seemed to be working. At one point he was given only two months to live.

125

Since Randy was a radiant Christian, I looked him up one day and asked him to go to the hospital with me to call on a young mother who was dying of cancer. I still remember the pointed question which he asked on the way, "Do you think it is right for a person like me to have a date?"

It was not just concern for the possibility that somehow his cancer might be contagious that he asked this question, but more specifically, should he be seeking relationships when he had such little time to live? Would it be fair to someone he might come to love? Would it be fair to himself?

As Randy continued to cling to life his health somehow improved. Ultimately, he became my associate and we worked together in the same church. He even lived for a time with our family and we became the closest of friends. His deliverance from cancer is certainly "providential" and possibly even "miraculous." In either case, to God be the glory!

On two different occasions I have been asked to write letters of recommendation for Randy. Each time the questionnaire asked for Randy's strong points I listed maturity. A young man who faces death in his late teens somehow grows up a little faster than do others.

This interesting fact brings us abruptly to the subject of prayer. As a young high school student, Randy was told by his sister that if he really wanted to grow in Christ he would have to pray for trials. Randy did really want to grow in Christ . . . so he prayed for trials.

It was only years later, after his amazing recovery from cancer, that he put two and two together and associated his prayers with his illness.

God does not cause illness. Illness comes from the Devil. But the Devil cannot do his evil work without God's permission. It was only after a consultation with God that the Devil was able to take away Job's wealth, or his health. Randy believes that the same was true with him. God did not cause him to be sick, but he allowed it. Randy now thinks that these trials came in answer to his prayers.

Be careful how you pray!

HOLLIS WHITROCK

Some time ago it was my privilege to meet Hollis Whitrock. At the time he was preaching in Colorado.

I was interested to discover that this eloquent and capable preacher of the Gospel had no formal theological training. The process by which God made a preacher out of Brother Whitrock gives us profound insights into the subject of prayer.

Hollis was working as a fireman and was doing contracting on the side. He felt a burden to be more active in Christian work, but lacked the courage to give up the job security and benefits of working for the fire department.

On more than one occasion he drove his pickup to the chief's office, fully intending to hand in his resignation. Each time, however, he lacked the faith and courage to go through with it.

Finally, in desperation, he prayed for God to get him out of that job. That, my friends, was a dangerous thing to do. In a very short time Hollis became ill . . . so ill in fact, that at one point he was given less than 30 days to live.

Not only was Hollis Whitrock not able to continue working for the fire department, he was not able to work at all. His wife found work to support the family and he tried to take care of the cooking and housework. His health was so bad, however, that he could not even go from room to room without crawling on the floor.

Finally, he gathered his family together and moved to Colorado. He was moving there to die.

As he planned a heritage for his children, be became more and more active in the church. He didn't want to leave his children in a youth group that was weak and unspiritual so he began ministering to them in his home.

Unexpectedly, his health began to improve. In about two years he was placed on staff by the church as a full-time youth worker and he continues in Christian work to this time.

Skeptics may deny any association between his prayers and his illness. Hollis Whitrock, however, feels differently.

I must emphasize that a life of Christian service is not filled with drudgery and regret. It is, in fact, life abundant. It is joy unspeakable and full of glory. It is exciting beyond words to work in the harvest fields for Jesus.

Therefore, it is not in any way dangerous spiritually for one to pray. We who are evil know how to give good gifts unto our children. They can ask for anything they want, but we who love them will only give them that which is ultimately appropriate for their own good.

From a carnal point of view, however, it is still sometimes dangerous to pray. God may choose to thrust us out into the harvest so that we can help to answer our own prayers.

DESTINED TO GLORIFY GOD

In John 9 is the story of a blind man whom Jesus healed. Jesus said that his destiny was to make manifest the works of God. It is interesting that no one else seemed to see him in this regard.

The disciples saw him theologically and wanted to know who sinned to place him in such a predicament.

The neighbors saw him socially as merely a beggar pleading for help.

The Pharisees saw him legally as involved in an infraction of the Sabbath Law.

His parents saw him emotionally . . . and even fearfully. Their statements regarding their son were framed in such a way that they would not be put out of the synagogue for the Scriptures teach that they "feared the Jews."

Jesus saw him differently! He saw him as a man whom God was going to use. The pain and problems of his life would be beautifully orchestrated by God to bring glory to His wonderful name. The Devil would be helpless to change the course of destiny, for God is capable of making even the errors and sins of mankind work out ultimately for good.

The greatest achievement of the Devil is seen at Calvary . . . and this, God has transformed into the best news the world has ever heard . . . or ever will hear.

Let me challenge you with the idea that you too have been born with a destiny to bring glory to God. Before you were born He knew you while you were yet in your mother's womb. He traced your steps throughout each precious moment up to the very present time. As you read these words, He is discerning the thought and intents of your heart.

He wants to guide you! Out of His infinite storehouse He longs to share bits of information and wisdom with you which will enrich your life and magnify your ministry.

GUIDED WITH HIS EYE

In Psalms 32:8 the Scriptures teach, "I will instruct thee and teach thee in the way which thou shalt go: I will guide thee with mine eye."

The next verse presents a dramatic contrast,

Be not as the horse, or as the mule, which have no understanding; whose mouth must be held in with bit and bridle, lest they come near unto thee . . . (Ps. 32:9).

God wants to guide us with His eye . . . He does not want us to be like a horse or a mule.

God wants us to be sensitive to His leading in our lives . . . He does not want to beat us into submission or bring about unnecessary pain by jerking us around with bit and bridle.

The obedient child knows what to do at bedtime . . . with a glance of the eyes a loving father can send the obedient child to bed.

129

The child without an obedient heart will make the experience an unpleasant one for everyone concerned.

Be not as the horse and the mule which have no understanding. Remember also that we do not pray without assistance,

... for we know not what we should pray for as we ought: but the Spirit itself maketh intercession for us with groanings which cannot be uttered (Rom. 8:26).

Let us enter in boldly, therefore, into the holiest of all by the blood of Jesus!

MY PRAYER

I knelt to pray when day was done,
And prayed, "O Lord bless everyone
Lift from each saddened heart the pain;
And let the sick be well again."
And then I woke another day.
And carelessly went on my way.

The whole day long I did not try
To wipe a tear from any eye
I did not try to share the load
Of any one along the road;
I did not even go to see
The sick man just next door to me.

Yet, once again when day was done,
I prayed, "O Lord, bless every one."
But as I prayed, into my ear,
There came a voice that whispered clear;
"Pause friend, before you pray,
Whom have you tried to help today?"

God's sweetest blessings always go;
To hands that serve him here below;
And then I hid my face and cried,
"Forgive me, God, for I have lied;
If you will let me live but another day,
I will try to live the way I pray."

(Anonymous)

*The testimonies of Randy Carlson and Hollis Whitrock are available on video tape from Good News Productions Int. in Joplin, Missouri.

THOUGHT QUESTIONS FOR CHAPTER XI

1. What does it mean in Romans 8:26 that we do not know how to pray as we ought?
2. How does the Holy Spirit intercede in our behalf?
3. Why do Christians sometimes behave like the "horse and the mule"?
4. How is it possible for God to guide us with His eye?
5. Does God ever do for us the things which we can do for ourselves?
6. Was Paul's "thorn in the flesh" good or bad (II Cor. 12)?
7. Was the experience of Jesus at Calvary good or bad?
8. How is it possible for all things to work together for good to them that love God and are the called according to his purpose (Rom. 8:28)?
9. Would you ever knowingly give anything to your children which would hurt them?
10. Will God ever give things to His children that would harm us?

XII

THE NEW COVENANT

. . . Behold the days come, saith the Lord, when I will make a new covenant with the house of Israel and with the house of Judah . . . (Heb. 8:8).

Perhaps no subject in the Bible is more exciting, or misunderstood, than the New Covenant.

A proper understanding of this concept involves going "beyond the veil" in the truest sense of the word. It is intrinsically associated with "knowing" God and being "born again."

To "know" in the Biblical use of that word means to become intimate with so that a new life is produced. In this respect Adam "knew" his wife and she conceived and bare him a son named Cain (Gen. 4:1). When the Scriptures inform us that Joseph and Mary did not have sexual congress before the birth of Jesus, that truth is expressed in these words, ". . . and (Joseph) knew her not till she had brought forth her firstborn son: and he called his name Jesus . . ." (Matt. 1:25).

To "know" means to become intimate with so that a new life is produced. When Adam unveiled his wife and became intimate with her a new life was produced. It is precisely this terminology and imagery which the Scriptures use to communicate truths regarding the "new birth" and the "New Covenant."

It is not by accident that the church is called the "bride" of Christ. Those who belong to Jesus experience with Him the intimacy of the marriage union in a spiritual sense. We stand before Him with total submission and vulnerability recognizing that ". . . all things are naked and opened unto the eyes of him with whom we have to do . . ." (Heb. 4:13). The marriage commitment, however, is not one-sided. Not only does Jesus have unlimited access to our innermost being beyond the door, or veil, of our hearts, we also have boldness to enter beyond the veil into the innermost recesses of His heart. This concept involves the very essence of conversion.

Just as husbands and wives develop the ability to communicate "nonverbally," so also the devout believer gains insight and guidance which is not available to others. The believer can pray for wisdom with the absolute assurance that it will be received (James 1:5-8). But the Sword of the Spirit cuts both ways. With reference to those who do not believe, the Scriptures state, "Let not that man think that he shall receive anything of the Lord. . . ."

When we open our hearts to receive Christ, our bodies become temples of the Holy Spirit. It is no longer necessary for us to journey to Jerusalem to worship the Father, for He dwells by faith in the innermost chambers of our mind and heart. In ancient times He met with Israel between the outstretched wings of the cherubim. They were located on top of the Ark of the Covenant in the Holy of Holies. Today we have the privilege of making our own heart the ark of His blessed covenant where we can meet with Him at any moment of the day or night . . . and He has promised never to leave us or forsake us (Heb. 13:5).

Since a proper concept of the New Covenant strikes at the very heart of Christianity, permit me to take a few moments and try to correct some prevalent misconceptions.

For the past 1,500 years virtually all of Christendom has called the first 39 books of the Bible the "Old Testament" and the last 27 books of the Bible the "New Testament." This is not so! It never has been, and it never will be!

The Bible actually contains at least eight covenants or testaments. They are:

1. The Covenant with Adam - Hosea 6:7

2. The Covenant with Noah - Jer. 53:20, Gen. 9:9

3. The Covenant with Abraham - Gen. 12:1-3; Gal. 3:17

4. The Covenant of Circumcision - Acts 7:8

5. The Ten Commandments - Deut. 4:11-13, 5:1-3

6. The Covenant of Peace - Exod. 40:13-15; Num. 25:12-13

7. The Covenant with David - II Sam. 7:12-17; Jer. 33:20-21

8. The New Covenant - Heb. 8:8-13

When Alexander Campbell commented upon these covenants he observed that commands, promises, appointments and ordinances are all equally called "covenants" in the Scriptures. He further noted that every covenant mentioned in the Bible originated with God and not with man.

When the Holy Spirit, however, speaks of the Old Covenant, as opposed to the New Covenant, it is invariably done with reference to the Ten Commandments. In the language of Scripture, we may say emphatically that the Old Testament or Covenant is in fact the Ten Commandments and not the first 39 books of the Bible.

As proof of this, please consider the following:

1. There is not one verse of Scripture which ever refers to the first 39 books of the Bible as a Covenant or Testament.

2. The Scriptures teach that the Old Covenant was made when God took His people by the hand to lead them out of the land

of Egypt (Heb. 8:9). The Ten Commandments were given at this time but most of the inspired men whom God used to write our Bible were not even born when God took His people by the hand to lead them out of the land of Egypt.

3. God made a covenant with His people in Horeb (Deut. 5:2) or in the language of Galatians 4:25, "Mt. Sinai in Arabia." The first 39 books of the Bible, however, were not written in "Mt. Sinai in Arabia," but in Palestine, Babylon and Persia.

4. The Old Covenant had been broken by the time of Jeremiah. He stated so quite clearly in Jeremiah 31:32. Some books of the Hebrew Bible, however, were not yet written at this time.

5. The Scriptures teach explicitly that Moses received a covenant while he was 40 days upon Mt. Sinai; this covenant was written upon two tablets of stone; this covenant was called "The Ten Commandments"; and the Scriptures teach that once these Ten Commandments were completed, God "added no more" to them (Deut. 5:22). See also Exodus 34:27-28; Deuteronomy 4:11-13; 5:1-3; 9:11, etc.

6. Once the Ten Commandments were completed they were placed in a box, or receptacle, called the "Ark of the Covenant" (Num. 10:33, etc.).

Thus the logical mind is forced to the conclusion that the Old Testament or Covenant is the Ten Commandments and not the first 39 books of the Bible. This covenant was written in tablets of stone at the time when God took His people by the hand to lead them out of the land of Egypt. It was placed in the Ark of the Covenant which was normally kept in the Holy of Holies in the Tabernacle and Temple. It was the spiritual hub or focal point around which Hebrew worship revolved, and it was a covenant which Israel did not keep.

The Old Testament, that is the Ten Commandments, is allegorically presented to us in Scripture by reference to Ishmael and his mother, Hagar (Gal. 4:24). The Bible calls Ishmael a "wild man" and predicted that "his hand will be against every man, and every man's hand against him . . ." (Gen. 16:12).

136

Even the most cursory reflection upon the Ten Commandments will reveal their controversial nature and help us to understand why Ishmael is used to illustrate their impact upon society.

By way of illustration let us consider the shortest, and perhaps the most obvious and simple of the Ten Commandments, "Thou Shalt Not Kill." These four words seem so obvious and simple that on the surface it is difficult to imagine how they could ever be misunderstood or considered as controversial. We want to shout, "God said what He meant, and meant what he said" and let that be the end of it!

Unfortunately, however, that is not the end of it, and people begin to ask questions about what these four simple words mean.

Plants and animals are alive. Is it wrong to kill them? Most of us would think not, but there are a great many people in India who hold every form of life so sacred that they will not even step on an insect.

Even in the Christian community, however, there is a wide difference of opinion on capital punishment, military service, abortion, and war.

Since each of us is at a different stage of growth intellecually, socially and spiritually, it is doubtful if we will ever come to understand these four simple words in identically the same way.

Here is a simple test with only 25 questions. The extenuating circumstances, definitions, and controversies surrounding these questions are the stuff that legal libraries are made of. There are literally thousands of books which have been written to answer questions about the legal ramifications involving manslaughter and murder, and to this very date even the experts are not always agreed on what constitutes justifiable homicide.

After considering this little questionnaire I think you will discover that even the Christian community will not always agree on what "Thou shalt not kill" actually means.

TRUE OR FALSE

1. I can kill anyone who breaks into my house.
2. I can kill anyone who threatens my life, but not my property.

3. I can kill in defense of my family but not in self-defense.
4. I can kill in defense of my country.
5. I can become a police officer and kill in the line of duty.
6. Christians in Britain had every right to kill Argentinians over the Falkland Islands.
7. Christians in Argentina had every right to kill Britains over the Falkland Islands.
8. Capital punishment is ordained by God.
9. Treason is a capital offense.
10. The United States has every right to execute a person convicted of treason.
11. The Soviet Union has every right to execute a person convicted of treason.
12. English soldiers had every right to kill our forefathers for revolting against their king.
13. Our forefathers had every right to kill English soldiers in our struggle for independence.
14. Americans have every right to kill foreigners who invade our land.
15. The American Indians had every right to kill our ancestors who invaded their land.
16. "Savages" have no rights.
17. Since life begins at the moment of conception it is murder to use a form of "morning after" birth control.
18. Abortion is murder under any circumstance.
19. Abortion is permissible to save the mother's life.
20. Christians can kill animals and birds just for pleasure.
21. A Christian can only kill animals and birds if they are used for food.
22. It is more fun to shoot an animal with a gun than a camera.
23. Rape is a capital offense.
24. Adultery is a capital offense.
25. The words "Thou Shalt Not Kill" are clear and do not need to be interpreted.

I suggest for your thinking that our answers to these questions will not be identical unless we cease to think and allow someone else to answer all of these questions for us. As we develop and gain new insights and information we might conceivably even change our own minds on some particular point.

SO WHAT?

A study of the Old Covenant may seem far afield from the burning issues of modern life. We may be tempted to forget about the "covenant" as irrelevant to our personal needs and plunge into our problems with the feeling that with hard work and diligence we will somehow get the job done.

Unfortunately, sometimes we discover just the opposite. Sometimes the "hurrier we go, the behinder we get."

Our own personal problems and needs cannot be divorced or disassociated from our relationship with the church. The church is the Body of Christ. When we are born again we are added to the church. As members of His Body we are linked together in such a way that when one member suffers we are all affected by that pain (I Cor. 12:13-27).

In this regard we need to understand that a fully functioning, unified Body is the key to world evangelism and power. This is so precisely stated by Jesus in His High Priestly prayer of John 17, that the meaning ought to be obvious to all.

He prayed,

Neither pray I for these alone, (that is, not just for His Apostles) but for them also which shall believe on me through their word; that they all may be one; as thou Father, art in me, and I in thee, that they also may be one in us: that the world may believe that thou hast sent me . . . (John 17:20-21).

Today, however, believers are not united . . . and neither does the world believe. These two indisputable facts need to be seen together. We can never experience world evangelism and the ultimate expression of Christian power until believers are united.

139

Probing into this very problem brings us back to a study of covenants. This is so absolutely foundational to our relationship with God, and also with one another, that we must pursue it further.

The Old Covenant was written on tablets of stone. It was cold, rigid and inflexible. As we have pointed out, it was always the subject of debate and the focal point of division. We have mentioned "Thou Shalt Not Kill," but perhaps a more obvious source of controversy is the command to "Remember the Sabbath Day and keep it holy." Jewish scholars have debated this command for literally thousands of years and they are no closer to agreement now than when they began.

The point needs to be seen that literally everything written down becomes controversial when it is considered from a legal point of view.

I once attended a court proceding which resulted from an injury accident. A farm hand had fallen from a tractor and been run over by an implement. He had sustained permanent injury. If I understood the case correctly, the outcome hinged upon a technical interpretation of one small clause in the insurance policy. One attorney argued that the presence of a comma and not a semi-colon indicated that this injury was indeed covered by the insurance policy. In his judgment the two debated phrases were, therefore, definitely linked together. The other attorney countered with the argument that similar, if not identical, cases had already been debated before the legal system and a court precedent had been established to the contrary.

The judge took the case under advisement and I never heard the outcome. Regardless of how he renders judgment, however, someone will be mad.

God completely by-passed the argument, debate, and division with His New Covenant by not writing it down where other people could read it. He said,

> . . . for this is the covenant that I will make with the house of Israel after those days, saith the Lord: I will put my laws into their mind, and write them in their hearts . . . (Heb. 8:10).

God is without variation or shadow cast by turning, but we are not. God's Word remains eternally the same, but we do not. Every day for us is a day of transition. Our perception of God and His Holy Word is in a constant state of flux and change. From the moment we were born until the moment we die our hearts and minds are either developing or declining. Sometimes through injury or illness we suffer traumatic experiences which alter our view of almost everything.

In the Christian community debate is not a virtue, it is a sin. It is categorized as a work of the flesh and is not associated with the fruit of the Spirit (see Gal. 5:19-24).

THE NEW COVENANT

This brings us to consider the New Testament, or Covenant, and to emphatically point out that it is not the last 27 books of the Bible as many have assumed.

As proof of this please consider the following:

1. Not once do the Scriptures ever refer to the last 27 books of the Bible as a covenant or testament.

2. The Christian Scriptures were written with paper and ink (see II John 12; III John 13; etc.) but the New Covenant is not written with ink, but with the Spirit of the Living God (II Cor. 3:3).

3. The New Covenant became a reality on the first Pentecost following our Lord's resurrection. Thousands were saved and became covenant people, but it was years before the first words of New Testament Scripture were written.

4. The Scriptures came gradually as God guided inspired men into all truth. The canon of New Testament Scripture was not completed until near the end of the first century and was not generally accepted throughout Christendom until many years later. The oldest extant list of canonical books which corresponds to our own, dates back only to the fourth century. The New Covenant was a complete reality before one word of Christian Scripture was written and literally thousands of Christian

141

martyrs died as covenant people before John wrote the book of Revelation.

5. The Old Covenant was written upon tablets of stone, but the New Covenant is written upon the fleshly tables of the heart and in the inner workings of the mind (II Cor. 3:3; Heb. 8:8-10).

6. The Old Covenant was in the Tabernacle or Temple, but the New Covenant is in our hearts so that our bodies become temples of the Holy Spirit (I Cor. 6:19). Just as God's glory was associated with the Ark of the Covenant in Old Testament times, we also are to "glorify" God in our body and in our spirit which are the Lords.

I MUST STATE EMPHATICALLY, THAT,

ALL SCRIPTURE IS GIVEN BY INSPIRATION OF GOD, AND IS PROFITABLE FOR DOCTRINE, FOR REPROOF, FOR CORRECTION, FOR INSTRUCTION IN RIGHTEOUSNESS: THAT THE MAN OF GOD MAY BE PERFECT, THOROUGHLY FURNISHED UNTO ALL GOOD WORKS (II Tim. 3:16-17).

Nevertheless, the Scriptures are not the covenant, and to attempt to make them such would be to live a B.C. life in an A.D. world.

If we make the mistake of considering the Christian Scriptures as the New Covenant then we will face the same divisive problems with them that the Jews did with the Ten Commandments.

Take, for example, the qualifications for a bishop which are recorded in I Timothy 3. Let us consider verse 2 and the expression "husband of one wife." The Greek words so translated mean literally "one woman man."

Again I will burden you with a brief questionnaire and the absolute assurance of controversy if you choose to pursue these words from a legal point of view.

TRUE OR FALSE

1. A bachelor cannot in any circumstance be a bishop.
2. A man who is divorced cannot in any circumstance be a bishop.

3. A man may become a bishop if he was divorced before becoming a Christian.
4. A man may remain a bishop if his wife leaves him.
5. A man who has had pre-marital sex cannot be a bishop.
6. A divorced man cannot be a bishop but a man with an annulled marriage can.
7. If a bishop's wife dies he must resign.
8. If a bishop's wife dies he must resign if he remarries.
9. A man who has been unfaithful to his wife can never be a bishop.
10. A secret affair might not disqualify a bishop if he repents.
11. The words "one woman man" have nothing to do with homosexuality.
12. A bishop can have a homosexual affair and still be a "one woman man."
13. A bishop who commits adultery in his heart should resign.
14. The qualifications of a bishop were mainly given to exclude polygamy.
15. The qualifications of a bishop were mainly given to exclude adultery.
16. These qualifications mean only that a bishop can have only one wife at a time.
17. Sexual sins committed before becoming a Christian do not affect a man's qualifications to be a bishop.
18. It is impossible to give a blanket statement regarding sexual sins that involve the qualifications of a bishop.
19. A man who loves only one woman can still be a bishop even though he does not marry her.
20. This qualification should not be construed as requiring marriage, only excluding promiscuity.
21. A polygamist cannot be a Christian.
22. Paul was not qualified to be a bishop.
23. If Paul was once married and his wife was dead he would be qualified to be a bishop.
24. The qualifications of a bishop are more strict than the qualifications for an apostle.

25. The qualifications for a bishop are clear and do not need to be interpreted.

The Old Testament is allegorically presented to us in Scripture by Hagar and Ishmael. It was a fleshly and carnal relationship that brought about disputes and endless controversies. Remember Genesis 16:12 which teaches that Ishmael ". . . will be a wild man; his hand will be against every man, and every man's hand against him . . ."

The New Covenant, by contrast, is allegorized by Sarah and Isaac. The name Isaac means "laughter." His birth and his very nature are supernatural and transcendent. Christians are not to be distinguished by controversy, but by love. Jesus said, "By this shall all men know that you are my disciples if you have love one to the other" (John 13:35).

SYNERGY

Synergy is defined as "The joint action of agents so that their combined effect is greater than the algebraic sum of their individual effect."

R. Buckminister Fuller provides this illustration in his book, *Synergetics,* which was published by MacMillan Publishing Company.

Note the tensile strength of the following commercially available metals:

Iron	60,000 lbs. p.s.i.
Chromium	70,000 lbs. p.s.i.
Nickel	80,000 lbs. p.s.i.
Carbon	50,000 lbs. p.s.i.

Total mathematical strength of these metals	260,000 lbs. p.s.i.
Strength of chrome nickel steel alloy	350,000 lbs. p.s.i.

This is the principle of synergy. If you consider these four metals as links in a chain, the chain will be no stronger than its weakest link and will fail at 50,000 lbs. p.s.i. which is the strength of carbon.

If you consider these four metals as strands woven into a cable, you add their combined strengths together and come up with 260,000 lbs. p.s.i.

The synergic concept, however, transcends either illustration. When these four metals are melted together so that each loses its own identity, a brand new metal is formed. The chrome nickel steel alloy is stronger than the algebraic sum of its individual parts.

There is a sense in which we also as Christians gain new power when we die to self and lose our own identity. When the Holy Spirit melts us into oneness with Jesus, we also become one with every other believer who shares with Him the intimacy of the New Covenant.

When you pray for something as an individual it is somehow different from two or three people coming to "agree" in prayer.

The Holy Spirit invites you to enter in boldly beyond the veil by the blood of Jesus Christ.

I just wanted to prepare you for the possibility that you might encounter others in the Holy of Holies with God that you might not expect to see there.

THOUGHT QUESTIONS FOR CHAPTER XII

1. What was the Old Covenant?
2. Where was it kept?
3. Why was it the object of disagreement and controversy?
4. What is the New Covenant?
5. Where is it located?
6. How does it avoid disagreement and controversy?
7. How might a misunderstanding of the New Covenant result in division?
8. How is Christian unity associated with world evangelism?
9. Why did Jewish people fear to go beyond the veil?
10. Where do Christians get boldness to enter beyond the veil?

XIII

GREATER WORKS THAN THESE

Verily, verily, I say unto you, He that believeth on me, the works that I do shall he do also; and greater works than these shall he do; because I go unto my Father (John 14:12).

When Jesus was upon the earth He performed all sorts of physical miracles. He gave sight to the blind, healed the sick, raised the dead, multiplied the loaves and fish, and in many other ways manifested that which was supernatural in the presence of those around Him.

He promised that His followers who believed in Him would do these things also.

But He also promised that they would do "greater" things because He was going unto the Father.

I have a growing conviction that these "greater" things do not refer to physical miracles. Jesus fed 5,000 men and their families with only five loaves of bread and two small fish. How can someone do a greater miracle than this? Do we have to feed 10,000 men with four loaves and one fish? I think not!

In order to understand these words I think we have to place physical things in their proper perspective.

THE THINGS WHICH WE SEE ARE TEMPORAL

". . . For the things which are seen are temporal; but the things which are not seen are eternal . . ." (II Cor. 4:18).

When Jesus multiplied the loaves and fish He was working with things that were only temporal. They picked up the fragments that were left over, but their value would be short-lived. How long will unrefrigerated fish remain edible? How long will bread be good to eat? The multitudes who ate and were satisfied would be hungry again in only a few short hours.

Jesus said to the Samaritan woman at Jacob's well, ". . . Whosoever drinketh of this water shall thirst again" (John 4:13). Water, which is so necessary to physical life, is temporal and transitory. Spilled upon the ground it will disappear in a few short minutes. Imbibed by a human being it will soon be absorbed into our system and thirst will again return.

Jesus sought to point us to spiritual treasures. He spoke of water which will cause us to never thirst again. He promised treasures which moth and rust cannot corrupt and which thieves cannot break through and steal. These promises obviously deal with the spiritual, and it is here that believers are privileged to do "greater" works because Jesus went to the Father.

The same truth is stated again in John 7:38-39.

> He that believeth on me, as the Scripture hath said, out of his belly shall flow rivers of living water. (But this spake he of the Spirit, which they that believe on him should receive: for the Holy Spirit was not yet given; because that Jesus was not yet glorified).

While Jesus was in His physical body He could only be one place at a time. When He was in Jerusalem He could not be also at Capernaum, and vice versa. When He was spending time with Jairus' daughter He could not also be spending time with blind Bartimaeus.

For this reason He said,

It is expedient for you that I go away: for if I go not away, the Comforter will not come unto you; but if I depart, I will send him unto you . . . (John 16:7).

The things which we see are temporal. Even the physical body of Jesus was temporal. When Jesus died and returned to the Father, He came back to earth in the "form" of a Spirit. As a Spirit He could be everywhere at the same time. He could be with all people who desired fellowship with Him, and He could be in all places simultaneously.

The greatest miracles are spiritual and not physical . . . for the things which we can see are only temporal.

JOHN THE BAPTIST

The contemporaries of Jesus knew that, "John did no miracle . . ." (John 10:41). Yet, Jesus said of him, "Among them that are born of women there hath not risen a greater than John the Baptist" (Matt. 11:11). Then He added immediately, "notwithstanding he that is least in the kingdom of heaven is greater than he."

These thoughts are so profound that we must summon all of our spiritual energies in an attempt to understand them. The Scriptures mention stupendous miracles performed by the prophets. Moses was used by God to bring ten plagues upon Egypt. Each of these miracles was of such magnitude that it influenced an entire nation of people. By the power of God, he parted the Red Sea and fed several million people for forty years in the wilderness. Elijah defeated the priests of Baal, started and stopped a three year drought, and was taken bodily into heaven. Elisha parted the Jordan, raised the dead, blinded

149

the Syrian army, and possessed such power that years after his death a dead man was revived by merely touching his bones.

Yet, in the eyes of God not one of these prophets was greater than John, even though John worked no miracle. Surely God sees things from a different perspective than man.

In order for the child of God to do "greater" works than Jesus he does not have to raise the dead, or cleanse the leper, or heal the sick. John the Baptist did not do these things and yet he was not inferior to any prophet that had been born of woman.

Yet, the least in the Kingdom of Heaven is greater than John!

HELEN KELLER

Helen Keller was born in Tuscumbia, Alabama. At the age of 19 months she suffered a terrible illness which left her blind, deaf, and dumb. This triple handicap made it virtually impossible for her to adequately appreciate much of the physical world around her. She could feel the warmth of the sun, but could not drink in the glorious beauty of a sunset. She could feel the bite of winter's snow, but could not see the beauty of a snow crowned mountain.

Her ability to "hear" was only by means of faint vibrations. When Enrico Caruso sang for her, she placed her fingers upon his lips. However inadequate was her perception of music, it was the best that she could do. She "heard" the music of Jascha Heifetz with her fingers resting lightly upon his violin, and when Feodor Chaliapin wanted her to hear his voice he placed his arm around her tightly and sang the "Volga Boat Song."

Her ability to speak has been called the greatest individual achievement in the history of education. Yet, she acknowledged that she had only partially conquered the hostile silence which imprisoned her. She said,

My voice is not a pleasant one, I am afraid, but I have clothed its broken wings in the unfailing hues of my dreams and my

150

struggle for it has strengthened every fiber of my being and deepened my understanding of all human strivings and disappointed ambitions.

The normal human being has five senses. We can touch, hear, see, taste, and smell. Each of these abilities deals only with the physical. You cannot touch, hear, see, taste, or smell a spirit. We live in a universe which is literally filled with spiritual realities that we have almost no way of perceiving. Whatever faint vibrations which we feel can excite our interest and inspire our imagination, but cannot do justice to the beauty and power of those spiritual beings around us.

In this regard, consider again the prayer of Paul for the Ephesians. He wanted God to open the eyes of their understanding,

> . . . that ye may know what is the hope of his calling, and what the riches of the glory of his inheritance in the saints, and what is the exceeding greatness of his power to us-ward who believe . . . (Eph. 1:18-19).

The realities are there, but we can never start to appreciate the "greater" works about which Jesus spoke until we see them.

HEAVENLY PLACES

The expression "heavenly places" occurs five times in the book of Ephesians. The word "places" is in italics, which means that it is not in the original text. Some have, therefore, translated it as "heavenlies." Perhaps it refers to the invisible world of eternal spirits which one must be born again in order to see. At any rate, it is the very focal point of Christian warfare, for the Scriptures teach that we wrestle not against flesh and blood, but against principalities, powers, rulers of the darkness of this world, and against spiritual hosts in the heavenlies (Eph. 6:12).

At the time Paul wrote these inspired words he was in prison. From an earthly perspective he was a "loser" but he constantly described himself as "more than a conqueror." At the very time he was chained as a prisoner to a Roman soldier he was simultaneously sitting with Christ in the heavenlies (Eph. 1:3). The Devil is described as the god of this world (II Cor. 4:4), but at the same time Christ reigns at the right hand of God in the heavenlies (Eph. 1:20). We came out of the waters of Christian baptism to face the trials and temptations of a lost world, but at the same time we were raised up to sit with Christ in the heavenlies (Eph. 2:6). We cannot see the spirit world with human eyes, but the spirit world can see us. They behold our every action. We are indeed compassed about with a great cloud of witnesses, and it is in the church that they see the manifold wisdom of God being made manifest (Eph. 3:10).

In the world we may have tribulation, but we reign as kings in the world of the spirits.

Be of good cheer. Christ has overcome the world!

A GOOD REPORT THROUGH FAITH

The eleventh chapter of Hebrews is called the "faith chapter" of the Bible. In this chapter is a list of the heroes and heroines of the faith who through faith,

> subdued kingdoms, wrought righteousness, obtained promises, stopped the mouths of lions, quenched the violence of fire, escaped the edge of the sword, out of weakness were made strong, waxed valiant in fight, turned to flight the armies of the aliens. Women received their dead raised to life again . . . (Heb. 11:33-35).

The Scriptures then list another catalog of faithful witnesses who did not receive deliverance,

> . . . and others were tortured, not accepting deliverance; that they might obtain a better resurrection: and others had trial of cruel mockings and scourgings, yea, moreover of bonds and imprisonment: They were stoned, they were sawn asunder, were tempted, were slain with the sword: they wandered about in

sheepskins and goatskins; being destitute, afflicted, tormented; (Of whom the world was not worthy:) they wandered in deserts, and in mountains, and in dens and caves of the earth . . . (Heb. 11:35-38).

Before us we have what seems to be two groups of people. One had answers to their prayers and one who apparently did not. One group was delivered from the mouths of lions, and the other group was killed by lions. One group who turned to flight and armies of aliens, and another group who was chased about to seek refuge in dens and caves of the earth.

God, however, does not see these as two separate groups. He sees them as one. The Scriptures teach that, "THESE ALL, HAVING OBTAINED A GOOD REPORT THROUGH FAITH, RECEIVED NOT THE PROMISE . . ." (Heb. 11:39). Praise God! They were all faithful until death and received the crown of life!

FAITHFUL, NOT SUCCESSFUL

Some of you who read these words have demonstrated an unswerving loyalty to Christ. You have been faithful "in season and out of season," but your Sunday school class has not grown, your church has not been blessed with a lot of additions, your efforts at personal evangelism seem to be futile.

Cheer up! You can still be more than conquerors through Him that loved us. God calls us to be faithful, not successful.

Even Jesus did not go to the cross as "successful" by the standards of this world. The fickle multitudes that shouted "Hosanna to the son of David," shouted "crucify him" just a few days later. Even His disciples forsook Him and fled.

Who, by human standards, would have considered Him a King? Yet, it was by the very act of His death that He overcame the wicked one.

The first one who profited by the experience of Calvary was the last one whom the world would have chosen. Pilate had washed his hands of the matter; the Roman soldiers were gambling for His garments; the fickle mob passed by wagging their heads; the priests railed on Him in unbelief; but the lowly thief cried out, "Lord, remember me when thou comest into thy kingdom" (Luke 23:42).

The Scriptures indicate that he did not have long to wait. Jesus said, "Verily I say unto thee, Today shalt thou be with me in paradise" (Luke 23:43).

May the God of all mercy grant you the spiritual vision of that dying thief that you may enter with Him eternally . . . "beyond the veil . . ."

> Now unto him that is able to keep you from falling, and to present you faultless before the presence of his glory with exceeding joy, to the only wise God our Saviour, be glory and majesty, dominion and power, both now and ever. Amen (Jude 24).

THOUGHT QUESTIONS FOR CHAPTER XIII

1. Elijah worked miracles; John the Baptist did not. Who had the greatest faith?
2. Why did John the Baptist not work miracles?
3. Why did Jesus say that no one born of woman was greater than John the Baptist?
4. How is the least in the kingdom greater than John?
5. Do you know of anyone who has worked greater physical miracles than Jesus?
6. What did Jesus mean by "greater works than these shall he do; because I go unto my Father . . ."?
7. How is it possible to lay up treasure where moth and rust cannot corrupt, and where thieves cannot break through and steal?
8. Why does one have to be "born again" to see the Kingdom of Heaven?
9. Who would object if you opened your heart to receive Christ?
10. If you have not received Jesus Christ as your Lord, why don't you do it now?

EPILOGUE

MOUNTAINTOP EXPERIENCES

Harvey Bacus was a missionary for many years in the Caribbean. "Down there," he says, "the small island mentality" is a proverbial expression for people with a limited perspective.

He tells of an acquaintance who was born and raised on Grand Cayman Island. Grand Cayman is only 21 miles long and 7 miles wide. The highest point of land on the entire island is only 35 feet above sea level. Not only had this good sister never been off the island of her birth, she had never even been to that part of her homeland which boasted a 35 foot "mountain." She had a limited perspective indeed.

At the age of 50 she was flown to Kingston, Jamaica, for medical treatment. Harvey met her at the airport. It was night. "What are all those lights doing up in the sky?" she inquired. Harvey had to explain that those were houses . . . and that they

155

were not "up in the sky" but built upon the small mountains surrounding Kingston.

It is not my purpose to belittle this good woman who through no fault of her own had never seen a mountain. It is only to point out that in retrospect, "mountaintop" experiences are relative things. A native of Grand Cayman could "blow his mind" by standing on a 40 foot ladder. By visiting Jamaica, he could see the world from mountains that towers some 7,000 feet into the sky.

But even 7,000 foot mountains pale into insignificance for people who live in Colorado. I have a good friend who lives in Colorado Springs. The snow crowned summit of Pike's Peak is beautifully framed by the picture window in his living room. Within five short years of moving there the beauty and wonder of that majestic mountain had lost its magic for him, and he thought no more about it than the citizens of Grand Cayman Island did about a 35 foot mound of earth.

Mountaintop experiences are relative things indeed. I am told that the highest mountain on earth is Mt. Everest which towers some 29,000 feet above sea level. Should you ever be privileged to scale that mountain, your perspective would pale into insignificance by comparison with military pilots who fly routine missions at more than twice that height. Even our astronauts in orbit around our planet must bow their knee to those select few who have walked upon the moon.

At this particular point in time we are tempted to view a perspective from the moon as the "ultimate" pinnacle of human observation. I doubt it! It was indeed a "giant step" for mankind, but only a step. Only another milestone in man's reach for the stars.

There is, of course, a spiritual application to these truths. Our journey to glory does not come in one gigantic leap. We grow progressively from "one degree of glory to another" (II Cor. 3:18).

Each mountaintop we climb seems at the time to be the ultimate pinnacle of life. From that perspective we are prone to look down on others who stand on lesser levels and wonder why they do not see the things that we see. It is humbling to realize that somewhere there are always others looking down at us and wondering why we do not see the things that they see.

There is a sense in which all of our human experience bears identically the same relationship to our Infinite God.

One times 0 is the same as 1,000 times 0 or 1,000,000 times 0. Thus, the spiritual experience of a ten year old child bears the same relationship to our Infinite God as that of the world's greatest Christian. As a matter of fact, that ten year old child may be the world's greatest Christian.

You are important to God beyond my limited ability to understand, or to explain. Even the very hairs of your head are all numbered. God has watched your spiritual development with understanding, interest, and love. He has taken note of your interest in this book and is fully aware of your thoughts and emotions as you read this final page. It is He who summons you into His presence where you will climb new heights, gain new power, and have new perspectives.

Let us, therefore, enter in boldly into the Holiest by the blood of Jesus, by a new and living way, which He hath consecrated for us, through the veil, that is to say, His flesh.